W9-BNI-815

Living in the USA

1 A competency-based novel for beginning intermediate students of English

Judy Burghart

EDGEBROOK COMMUNITY CENTER
1926 Edgebrook Dr.
Apt. 1-B
Palatine, IL 60074
708/776-2523
Greens Apartments

National Textbook Company
a division of *NTC Publishing Group* • Lincolnwood, Illinois USA

To Catalina Paige

Project Editor:	Kathleen Schultz
Designer:	Linda Snow Shum
Cover and interior illustrations:	Sandra Burton

1994 Printing

Published by National Textbook Company, a division of NTC Publishing Group.
© 1990 by NTC Publishing Group, 4255 West Touhy Avenue,
Lincolnwood (Chicago), Illinois 60646-1975 U.S.A.
Manufactured in the United States of America.

4 5 6 7 8 9 VP 9 8 7 6 5

Contents

Introduction   v

Life Skills Chart   vi

Meet the Parkers   1

Chapter 1
Blue Bedroom Walls   2

Chapter 2
Only Crutches   10

Chapter 3
Welcome Back   20

Chapter 4
The Pigsty   28

Chapter 5
Don't Chew on the Right Side   38

Chapter 6
The Money Saver   46

Chapter 7
One More Dollar   56

Chapter 8
She's Going to Be Fifty   66

Chapter 9
First Class to Chicago   74

Chapter 10
Dial "9" First   84

Chapter 11
Passengers Only at This Point   94

Chapter 12
Go Straight and Turn Right   104

Chapter 13
Onions Make You Snore   114

Chapter 14
At the Amusement Park   122

Chapter 15
A Couple of Minutes Before Midnight   132

Introduction

Living in the U.S.A. is a three-book series of competency-based novels for young adult and adult students of English at the beginning intermediate, intermediate, and advanced intermediate levels. These novels are designed to meet students' specific needs in two separate, but equally important, areas—survival skills and language skills. The series reinforces and enhances the competencies that are taught in the adult English language classroom while presenting students with the type of developmental and consequential events that characterize a novel.

Students are introduced to the main characters, Ted and Janet Parker, and are invited to share their experiences in a series of everyday situations. Each chapter focuses on a specific event and includes a practical "how-to" solution for a common problem or issue the Parkers confront and resolve.

The general competencies explored include such issues as housing, health, employment, consumer education, money skills, clothing, transportation, community resources, home safety, legal rights, and government and law. Through Ted and Janet Parker, students will learn about specific life skills such as understanding store coupons, entering an emergency clinic, understanding a time card, using the newspaper, understanding fire hazards in the home, reading a bus schedule, using the state unemployment office, opening a checking account, and reporting a burglary.

The **Living in the U.S.A.** series is also a carefully graded course of grammar, vocabulary, and idioms. The exercises at the end of each chapter emphasize all four language skills and offer students an enjoyable way to relate the important places and events they are reading about to their own daily lives.

Life Skills Chart

Chapter	Specific Competencies
Chapter 1 **Blue Bedroom Walls**	• Using household tools • Understanding painting procedures
Chapter 2 **Only Crutches**	• Entering an emergency clinic • Talking to a doctor
Chapter 3 **Welcome Back**	• Understanding time cards • Understanding sick leave • Calling in sick
Chapter 4 **The Pigsty**	• Using household cleaning products
Chapter 5 **Don't Chew on the Right Side**	• Understanding dental health • Talking to a dentist
Chapter 6 **The Money Saver**	• Saving money • Understanding coupons
Chapter 7 **One More Dollar**	• Counting/giving change
Chapter 8 **She's Going to Be Fifty**	• Shopping for clothes • Talking with a salesclerk

General Competency	Grammar
Housing	• Present continuous • **To be** negative short answers • Using contractions • **Want** vs. **want to**
Health	• Present 3rd person singular • **Want/want to** vs. **need/need to** • Present short answers
Employment	• Present questions and negatives • Present vs. present continuous
Housing	• **Going to** (future) • **Want to** vs. **would like to** • Mixed short answers
Health	• Spelling - final **y** • Imperatives
Consumer Education	• Demonstratives • Present vs. Continuous vs. **going to**
Money Skills	• **There is/there are** • Contractions
Clothing	• Spelling - **es** and **ves** • **There was/there were** • Word order

Life Skills Chart

Chapter	Specific Competencies
Chapter 9 **First Class to Chicago**	• Sending parcel post vs. first class • Insuring a parcel • Understanding shipping rates
Chapter 10 **Dial "9" First**	• Understanding long distance collect calls • Identifying kinds of phone calls
Chapter 11 **Passengers Only at This Point**	• Understanding flight schedules • Understanding airport procedures
Chapter 12 **Go Straight and Turn Right**	• Reading highway signs • Giving directions
Chapter 13 **Onions Make You Snore**	• Using kitchen utensils • Fixing a snack
Chapter 14 **At the Amusement Park**	• Understanding admission • Understanding use of park grounds
Chapter 15 **A Couple of Minutes Before Midnight**	

General Competency	Grammar
Consumer Education	• Mixed tenses/**to be** • Modals
Consumer Education	• Mixed tenses • Word order
Transportation	• Regular past tense • Regular negative past plus negative past of **see** • **Any/anyone/anything** • Past short answers
Transportation	• Present/past questions • Impersonal expressions • Mixed tenses
Housing	• **A few/a little** • Regular past negative
Community Resources	• Past tense questions • **Much/many** • Past of **go** and **see**
	• Grammar/vocabulary/idiom review

Meet the Parkers

This is Ted Parker and this is Janet Parker. They're a young married couple and they live in San Diego, California. They live in an apartment.

Ted works for Sun Valley Fruit Company. He's an assistant manager and works in the office. Janet works for a store that sells computers. She's a salesperson and she works part-time.

Ted loves sports. He likes to golf, jog, and play baseball. Janet loves romantic movies. She likes to watch old movies on TV. Sometimes she goes jogging with Ted.

Ted and Janet are home now. It's Saturday. Do you want to meet them? We need to go to the Parker's apartment and see what they're doing this morning.

CHAPTER 1

Blue
Bedroom Walls

Vocabulary

furniture (n)   chairs, tables, desks, sofas, etc.

ladder (n)   a metal or wood frame used for climbing

messy (adj)   dirty or not in order

neat (adj)   clean or in order

roller (n)   a rolled tool used for painting

stir (v)   mix

tray (n)   a flat container used for holding things

Idioms

Ted wants to **take a break.**   stop working and rest

Ted is pushing the furniture **away from** the walls.   separated, not touching

Do you want to **make something to eat?**   prepare food

Blue Bedroom Walls

It's Saturday morning. Ted and Janet want to paint their bedroom today. They want blue bedroom walls, not white.

It's 9:00 A.M. Ted is pushing the furniture away from the walls. Janet isn't. She's putting old sheets on the furniture. She wants to cover the furniture.

Now Ted's bringing in the ladder and the paint. Janet's not. She's getting the paint trays, paint rollers and paint brushes.

Now Ted's stirring the paint and pouring some into the paint trays. He's painting with a roller. Janet isn't. She's painting with a brush. She wants to paint the corners.

Ted and Janet are wearing old clothes. They're busy now, and Janet is very messy. She's dirty, but Ted isn't. He's neat and clean.

Ted and Janet are working hard. Janet says, "Don't forget. I want to paint the ceiling, too."

Now it's 10:30. Ted wants to take a break. He's tired and hungry and thirsty, but Janet's not. She wants to paint some more.

TED: I'm tired, Janet. Are you?

JANET: No, I'm not tired, Ted.

TED: Do you want to take a break?

JANET: No, honey. I want to paint some more.

TED: I'm thirsty, too. Are you?

JANET: No, I'm not.

TED: Are you sure? How about a soda or a glass of ice water?

JANET: No, Ted! I'm not thirsty. I want to finish painting.

TED: Well, are you hungry?

JANET: No, I'm not. Thank you.

TED: Really? Do you want a banana or a candy bar?

JANET: No, Ted! I'm not hungry and I'm not thirsty! I want to paint some more!

TED: I'm very hungry, Janet. Do you want to make something to eat for me?

JANET: Oh, Ted! Go into the kitchen and make a sandwich! I'm finishing this bedroom!

TED: Well, okay. I'm taking a break now.

JANET: Good!

Ted is in the kitchen. He's eating a tuna sandwich. Janet's in the bedroom. She's on the ladder now and she's painting the ceiling. Oh-oh. She's falling off the ladder. "Ahhhhhhhhh!" Now Ted's running to the bedroom. Janet's on the floor. She's holding her ankle. Ted wants to help her get up.

TED: Janet, honey. Are you okay?

JANET: No, I'm not, Ted. It's my ankle. It hurts.

TED: Okay, honey. Take it easy and let me help you. I'm taking you to an emergency clinic.

Exercises

A.   Answer the questions in complete sentences.

1. What do Ted and Janet want to do today?

2. It's 9:00 A.M. What's Ted doing with the furniture?

3. What's Janet doing with the sheets?

4. Who's messy and who's neat?

5. It's 10:30 A.M. Who's taking a break?

6. What's Ted eating?

7. What's happening to Janet?

8. Where's Ted taking Janet?

B.   Take one out   Read each of these word groups. Take out the word or words that do not belong.

1. painting, thirsty, tired, hungry

2. falling, staying, wearing, want to

3. dirty, fall, messy, neat

4. sheets, furniture, bring, ladder

5. brush, roller, busy, paint

C.   Present continuous   Complete each sentence with the correct form of the present continuous tense. Follow the example:

She __is painting__ the bedroom. (paint)

1. Ted _____ the paint. (stir)

2. They _____ a break. (take)

3. He _____ the furniture away from the walls. (move)

4. We _____ tuna sandwiches. (eat)

5. I _____ in the paint trays. (bring)

6. You and I _____ old clothes. (wear)

7. She _____ off the ladder. (fall)

8. Ted and Janet _____ rollers. (use)

9. You and Ted _____ the paint trays. (get)

10. I _____ hard. (work)

D.   Negative short answer   Answer these questions using two negative contractions if possible. Follow the example:

Is Janet thirsty? No, she isn't.

No, she's not.

1. Are you pushing the furniture away from the wall? (only one contraction)

2. Is Janet making something to eat?

3. Are you and Ted painting?

4. Are you helping me? (only one contraction)

5. Are Ted and Janet wearing new clothes?

6. Is her ankle okay?

7. Are the paint trays in the bedroom?

8. Is the furniture new?

9. Are you and Janet painting the kitchen?

10. Is Janet taking a break?

E. **Painting a room** Read sentences 1 and 2. What do you want to do next? Use numbers 3 through 9 to put the sentences in order.

_____ Use the paint roller to paint the walls.

__**1**__ Put on your old clothes.

_____ Cover the furniture with old sheets.

_____ After your break, paint some more.

_____ Paint the corners with a paint brush.

__**2**__ Push the furniture away from the walls.

_____ Stir the paint.

_____ Bring in the ladder, paint, roller, brush, and paint tray.

_____ Stop for a minute. Have a soda.

F. **Want/want to** Practice these exchanges with a partner. Use **want** or **want to**. Follow the example:

    A: Do you _____want_____ a sandwich?

    B: No. I ____want to____ paint some more.

1. **A:** Do you _____ a paint brush?

    B: No. I _____ use a roller.

2. **A:** Do you _____ a soda?

   B: No, thanks. I _____ drink a cup of coffee.

3. **A:** Do you _____ your new shirt?

   B: No. I _____ wear my old clothes.

4. **A:** Do you _____ white paint?

   B: No. I _____ paint the room blue.

5. **A:** Do you _____ an ambulance?

   B: No. I _____ go by car to an emergency clinic.

6. **A:** Do you _____ paint the bedroom?

   B: Yes. I _____ blue walls.

7. **A:** Do you _____ make something to eat?

   B: Yes. I _____ a tuna sandwich.

8. **A:** Do you _____ use blue paint?

   B: Yes. I _____ a blue bedroom.

9. **A:** Do you _____ wear your old clothes?

   B: Yes. I _____ my old shirt and pants.

10. **A:** Do you _____ go to the hospital?

    B: Yes. I _____ a doctor.

CHAPTER 2

Only Crutches

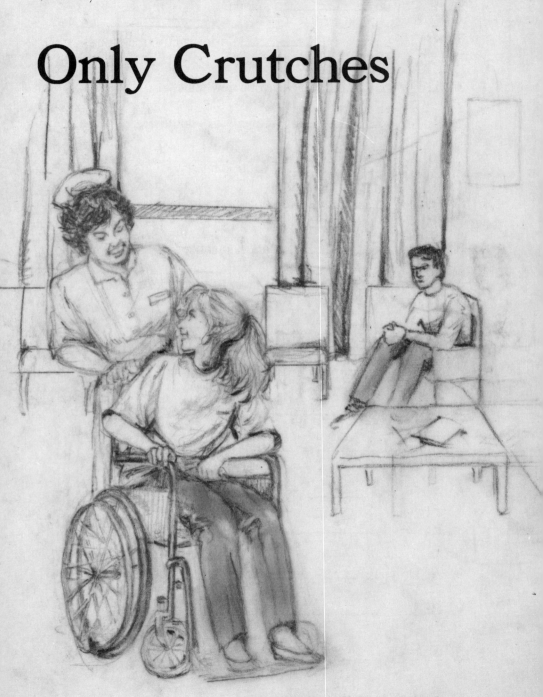

Vocabulary

crutches (n)   walking supports

medical form (n)   a paper that a patient needs to fill out

receptionist (n)   a person who receives people at the front desk

sprained (adj)   twisted and swollen

swollen (adj)   enlarged because of an injury

temperature (n)   hotness or coldness of the body

wheelchair (n)   a chair with wheels for a person who can't walk

Idioms

You need to **take it easy.**   rest, stay calm

You need to **fill out** this form.   complete

I want to **put** my foot **up.**   raise

Stay home for three or four days.   remain in the house

It's killing me.   It hurts.

I'm not doing very well.   I don't feel good.

Only Crutches

Janet and her husband are now at the emergency clinic. She has a very swollen ankle. Janet's sitting in a chair in the waiting room. Ted's getting the medical form from the receptionist.

"Here, honey," he says. "You need to fill out this form."

Janet fills out the medical form. She prints her name, address, phone number, work phone and social security number. She also gives information about her medical insurance. Then Janet signs her name. She gives the form back to Ted. Ted returns the form to the receptionist.

Now Ted and Janet are sitting in the waiting room. Janet's ankle hurts and Ted is a little nervous.

"Do you want to look at a magazine, Janet?" Ted asks.

"No thanks. I think I want to put my foot up. It's killing me." Janet puts her swollen foot up on a table.

In about fifteen minutes, a nurse comes with a wheelchair. Janet gets into the wheelchair and asks Ted, "Do you want to come with me to the examining room, or do you want to wait here?

"I think I want to wait here, honey," Ted answers.

Janet laughs. "Okay, you chicken," she says.

The nurse pushes Janet into the examining room. She takes Janet's temperature and blood pressure. Then the doctor takes X-rays of Janet's swollen ankle.

DR. KIM: Good morning, Janet. How are you today?

JANET: Morning. I'm not doing very well. My ankle really hurts. Is it broken?

DR. KIM: No, it isn't, Janet.

JANET: Are you sure?

DR. KIM: Well, look at your X-rays. See? You're lucky. It's only sprained.

JANET: What do I need to do for a sprained ankle? Do I need to use a wheelchair?

DR. KIM: No, you don't need a wheelchair. You need crutches to help you walk.

JANET: Only crutches? That's good. How about a bandage? Do you want to put a bandage on my ankle?

DR. KIM: Not now, Janet. Your ankle is very swollen. You need to put ice on it for twenty-four hours.

JANET: And then what happens?

DR. KIM: You need to take it easy and come back to see me in a week.

JANET: How about work?

DR. KIM: Stay home for three or four days. Keep your foot up. Don't walk on it and don't stand on it. Your husband needs to help you at home.

JANET: Really? That's terrific! He can cook dinner and clean the house and wash the clothes! Thanks, Dr. Kim!

Exercises

A.   Answer the questions in complete sentences.

1. What does Janet have?

2. Where are Ted and Janet now?

3. What does Janet need to fill out?

4. Where does Ted want to wait?

5. Where does the nurse push Janet?

6. What does the nurse take?

7. Is Janet's ankle broken?

8. What does Janet need? (not a wheelchair)

B. Multiple choice Choose **a, b** or **c** as the correct answer.

1. Janet's ankle is sprained. This means that her ankle is
    _____ .

    a. broken

    b. swollen

    c. crutches

2. Janet says, "It's killing me." This means that her ankle
    _____ .

    a. hurts

    b. is okay

    c. needs a bandage

3. Does Janet need a wheelchair? No. She needs _____ .

    a. an X-ray

    b. a medical form

    c. crutches

4. X-rays are _____ .

    a. temperatures

    b. blood pressure

    c. pictures of bones

5. The examining room is the room where _____ .

    a. the doctor looks at you

    b. you sign the medical form

    c. you fill out the medical form

6. The doctor says to Janet, "Keep your foot up." This means _____ .

    a. Janet needs to use crutches

    b. Janet needs to put a bandage on her ankle

    c. Janet needs to put her foot up on a table or chair

7. The doctor says, "Stay home for three or four days." This means _____ .

    a. Janet needs to go to work

    b. Janet cannot go to work

    c. Janet needs to sit down at work

8. The receptionist is the person who _____ .

    a. takes your X-rays

    b. gives you the medical form to fill out

    c. pushes you into the examining room

C.   Present tense   Complete each sentence with the verb in present tense. Use **s** or **es** for the third person singular. Follow the example:

Ted _____picks_____ Janet up and carries her. (pick)

1. Janet _____ information about her medical insurance. (give)

2. Janet _____ her foot up on a table. (put)

3. She _____ in the waiting room. (wait)

4. Her ankle _____ a lot. (hurt)

5. The nurse _____ Janet in a wheelchair. (push)

6. The doctor _____ Janet, "How are you today?" (ask)

7. His wife _____ crutches. (use)

8. Janet _____ to the doctor. (talk)

9. Her husband _____ to wait in the waiting room. (want)

10. Her husband _____ the clothes. (wash)

D.   Short story   Complete each sentence with the correct present tense form of **want, want to, need,** or **need to.**

Janet _wants to_ finish painting the bedroom, but she falls off the
(1)
ladder. Her ankle hurts. She _____ go to an emergency clinic.
(2)
She can't walk. Ted _____ drive her to the clinic.
(3)

"Do you _____ a magazine?" Ted asks.
       (4)

"No thanks," Janet says. "I _____ put my foot up."
                            (5)

The nurse comes with a wheelchair.

Janet asks Ted, "Do you _____ come with me or do you
                        (6)

_____ stay here?"
 (7)

The doctor says that Janet _____ crutches. He also says that
                            (8)

Janet _____ stay home for three or four days. She _____ Ted's
       (9)   (10)

help.

E. **Short answer**   Practice these exchanges with a partner.
Give the correct positive or negative present tense short answer.
Follow the example:

A: Do you want to wait here?

B: Yes, _____I do_____. I want to read a magazine.

1. A: Do I need a wheelchair?

   B: No, _____. You need crutches.

2. A: Do you want to put a bandage on it?

   B: No, _____. It needs ice.

3. A: Does your ankle hurt?

   B: Yes, _____. It hurts a lot.

4. **A:** Do Ted and Janet want to go to an emergency clinic?

   B: Yes, ——————. She needs a doctor.

5. **A:** Does Janet need crutches?

   B: Yes, ——————. Her ankle is sprained.

6. **A:** Does the nurse take X-rays?

   B: No, ——————. A doctor does.

7. **A:** Do I need to sign the medical form?

   B: Yes, ——————. Sign here, please.

8. **A:** Does Janet have a broken ankle?

   B: No, ——————. It's only sprained.

9. **A:** Do you and I need to go to the clinic?

   B: Yes, ——————. I can drive.

10. **A:** Does the doctor take her temperature and blood pressure?

    B: No, the doctor ——————. The nurse ——————.

F.   Dialogues   Practice one of these dialogues with a partner. Present it to the class.

Dialogue One

A: Good morning, ———. How are you today?

B: Morning. I'm not doing very well.

A: What's the matter?

B: My ankle hurts. I think it's sprained.

Dialogue Two

A: Do I need to use a wheelchair?

B: No, you need crutches to help you walk.

A: Do you want to put a bandage on my ankle?

B: No. Your ankle is very swollen. You need to put ice on it.

Dialogue Three

A: Do you want to look at a magazine?

B: No, I don't. I want to put my foot up.

A: I don't want to go to the examining room with you.

B: Okay, you chicken. You can sit here in the waiting room.

Dialogue Four

A: My ankle is killing me. Is it broken?

B: No, it isn't. It's only sprained.

A: I can't walk or stand on it.

B: Well, take it easy for three or four days.

CHAPTER 3

Welcome Back

Vocabulary

cover (v)   take care of or pay for (as sick leave)

illness (n)   sickness

time card (n)   the card that an employee uses for a time clock

time clock (n)   a clock that employees use to show their hours of work

wave (v)   use your hand to say hello to someone

Idioms

Welcome back.   a greeting that tells a person it is nice to see him or her return

She needs to **punch in (out).**   use a time card in a time clock

She needs to talk to you about your **sick leave.**   time off from work because of sickness

The cards are in **alphabetical order.**   in order of the alphabet (a,b,c)

You need to sign **a couple** of forms.   two, a pair

Welcome Back

Janet's ankle is feeling much better now, and she's going back to work. Janet's boss knows that she's returning today.

At work, Janet walks over to the time clock. She waves good morning to the other employees, and they welcome her back.

"Hi, Janet. Good to see you back. How's your ankle?" asks Bob.

"It's much better, thanks," answers Janet, "but I still need to wear a bandage. I'm glad I don't need crutches anymore." Janet waves to some other friends at work.

Now Janet's looking for her time card. She needs to punch in every morning. Every employee punches a time card. The workers punch in and out every morning and every afternoon. The secretary keeps a record of everyone's working hours.

Janet doesn't see her time card. The cards are always in alphabetical order, and Janet's card is always after Richard Orlando's card. But Janet doesn't see it.

Janet sees Richard. He's getting a cup of coffee. He gets a cup of coffee every morning. Most of the employees drink coffee.

"Hi, Richard!" Janet calls. "I don't see my time card here. Do you know anything about it?"

"I think the secretary has it. She needs to talk to you about your sick leave. She wants to see you right away."

"Thanks, Richard," says Janet. Now she's walking into the secretary's office. The secretary is busy. She's typing and answering the phone. Janet needs to wait a couple of minutes to talk to her.

MS. TAYLOR: Welcome back, Janet. How do you feel?

JANET: Much better, thank you. Do you need to see me?

MS. TAYLOR: That's right. It's about your sick leave. You need to sign a couple of forms for me. Then the company can pay you your sick time.

JANET: Sure. Where do I sign? Here?

Now Janet's signing the forms. Every employee signs the forms to get sick leave pay.

MS. TAYLOR: There's a problem, Janet. A small one.

JANET: What is it?

MS. TAYLOR: You don't have enough sick time to cover the four days of your illness.

JANET: How much sick leave do I have?

MS. TAYLOR: Three days. The company can pay you for three days only.

JANET: I understand. Well, I'm ready to go back to work now.

MS. TAYLOR: Good. Here's your time card. And take it easy on that ankle.

Exercises

A.   Answer the questions in complete sentences.

1. How is Janet's ankle now?

2. What does Janet need to do every morning at work?

3. In what order are the time cards?

4. What does the secretary need to talk to Janet about?

5. What does Janet need to do for the secretary?

6. What is the small problem?

7. For how many days can the company pay Janet for sick time?

8. What does the secretary give Janet?

B. Matching Match each group of words in **A** with a group of words in **B** to make a complete sentence. Write the letter of the correct answer on the line.

A	**B**
_____ 1. Welcome back, Janet. How	a. crutches anymore.
_____ 2. You don't have enough sick time	b. but she doesn't see it.
_____ 3. I'm glad I don't need	c. for three days only.
___g___ 4. Every employee	d. drink coffee.
___d___ 5. Most of the employees	e. a couple of forms for me.
_____ 6. Janet's looking for her time card	f. do you feel?
_____ 7. The company can pay you	g. punches a time card.
___e___ 8. You need to sign	h. to cover the four days of your illness.

C.   Present tense question   Complete each sentence with **do** or **does** and the main verb. Follow the examples:

___Does___ Janet ____drink____ coffee? (drink)

___Do___ they ___sign___ the forms? (sign)

1. _____ the secretary _____ the phone? (answer)

2. _____ Richard _____ coffee every morning? (have)

3. _____ the employees _____ sick leave? (get)

4. _____ the workers _____ in every morning?
   (punch)

5. _____ her ankle _____ better? (feel)

6. _____ the company _____ sick leave? (give)

7. _____ Richard and Janet _____ in the morning?
   (talk)

8. _____ the secretary _____ Janet's time card?
   (have)

9. _____ you _____ where her time card is? (know)

10. _____ I _____ to sign this form? (need)

D.   Present tense negative   Complete each sentence with **don't** or **doesn't** and the main verb. Follow the examples:

Janet ___doesn't drink___ coffee. (drink)

They ___don't sign___ the forms. (sign)

1. I _____ very well today. (feel)

2. She ＿＿＿＿＿＿＿ enough sick time to cover the four days of her illness. (have)

3. The boss ＿＿＿＿＿＿＿ any letters. (type)

4. The employees ＿＿＿＿＿＿＿ sick often. (get)

5. Her ankle ＿＿＿＿＿＿＿ swollen anymore. (look)

6. We ＿＿＿＿＿＿＿ where her time card is. (know)

7. The company ＿＿＿＿＿＿＿ the employees vacation with pay. (give)

8. Your sick leave ＿＿＿＿＿＿＿ this illness. (cover)

9. I ＿＿＿＿＿＿＿ the problem. (understand)

10. You ＿＿＿＿＿＿＿ to sign anything. (need)

E.   Present tense or present continuous   Complete each sentence with the present tense or the present continuous form of the verb. Follow the examples:

Janet ＿＿＿works＿＿＿ every day. (work)

Janet ＿＿is working＿＿ now. (work)

1. Janet ＿＿＿＿＿＿＿ in every morning. (punch)

2. She ＿＿＿＿＿＿＿ in now. (punch)

3. Richard ＿＿＿＿＿＿＿ coffee now. (drink)

4. Richard ＿＿＿＿＿＿＿ coffee every day. (drink)

5. We ＿＿＿＿＿＿＿ to our friends every morning. (wave)

6. Look out the window. It _____ now. (rain)

7. Ted and Janet _____ about her ankle now. (talk)

8. The secretary _____ everyone's time card in her office. (have)

9. The boss _____ Janet is returning to work today. (know)

10. I _____ a break now. (take)

F. Complete this dialogue with a partner. Practice talking to the secretary about your sick leave and your time card.

SECRETARY: Welcome back. I'm glad to see you again. How's your ankle?

YOU: My ankle is _____ . Thank you.

SECRETARY: There's a problem. A small one.

YOU: What _____ ?

SECRETARY: You don't have enough sick leave to cover the four days of your illness.

YOU: I see. How much _____ ?

SECRETARY: You only have three days of sick leave. The company can pay you for three days only.

YOU: Do you have _____ ?

SECRETARY: Yes, I do. I have your time card right here. And take it easy on that ankle.

YOU: Thank you very much.

CHAPTER 4

The Pigsty

Vocabulary

cleanser (n)   a product used to clean bathtubs and sinks

dust (v)   clean the dirt off the furniture

pigsty (n)   a dirty room, a place where pigs live

products (n)   items shoppers can buy at the supermarket or store

rag (n)   an old piece of clothing used for cleaning

sponge (n)   a cleaning item that can hold a lot of water

stuff (n)   things, belongings

Idioms

Janet is **wide awake.**   very awake, not sleepy

You win.   You are right.

Go ahead.   Do what you want.

I'm going to **take a nap.**   sleep for a short time

Our stuff is **all over.**   everywhere

The Pigsty

"This place is a pigsty!" Janet shouts to her husband early Saturday morning. "Look at this place! Clothes on the floor! Newspapers everywhere! Your running shoes! My make-up! A dirty bathroom! Our stuff is all over the place!"

It's only 7:30 and Ted wants to sleep some more. He doesn't want to look at their messy apartment.

"Janet, I'd like to sleep a little more," he says. "Can you be quiet, please?"

But Janet is wide awake. She wants to begin cleaning the apartment, and she'd like her husband to help.

"Get up, lazybones," Janet says. "I want to clean this place now before you leave for your Saturday morning golf game. Would you like to help me?"

Ted covers his face with the blanket. He wants to sleep. He would not like to help his wife—not at 7:30 on a Saturday morning. "No, I wouldn't," Ted says from under the blanket. "Go away, Janet, and let me sleep."

But Janet knows how to wake up her husband. She gets the vacuum cleaner and begins to vacuum the bedroom. She knows the noise is going to wake him up.

"And when he's awake, he's going to help me clean this mess," she says to herself.

It works. After five minutes of vacuuming, Ted gets up.

"Okay, honey," Ted says. "You win. What would you like me to do?"

JANET: First, I'd like you to put your dirty clothes in the laundry basket, and then I'd like you to dust the furniture.

TED: Okay. Where's the furniture polish?

JANET: It's under the kitchen sink with all of the other cleaning products.

TED: How about a rag? Do you want me to use a rag or a paper towel?

JANET: A rag. I'm going to clean the bathroom. Will you please bring me a sponge and the cleanser?

TED: Sure. Anything else? Like breakfast? How about some cold pizza from last night?

JANET: Go ahead. I'm going to finish cleaning this pigsty. Don't forget to dust the bookcase.

TED: Okay. I'm going to put the dirty dishes in the dishwasher. Are there any dirty dishes in the bedroom?

JANET: Yes, there are. The bowl from our popcorn last night and the glass from your soda.

TED: Would you like me to start the laundry, too?

JANET: No, honey. I'm going to do the laundry after I clean this messy bathroom.

TED: I'm going to take a break and eat breakfast.

JANET: I need the glass cleaner for the bathroom mirror. Would you bring it to me?

TED: Sure, honey. And do you know what? After we finish cleaning, I'm going to take a nap before golf!

Exercises

A.   Answer the questions in complete sentences.

1. Where is their stuff?

2. It's only 7:30. What does Ted want to do?

3. How does Janet wake Ted up?

4. Where would Janet like Ted to put his dirty clothes?

5. What is Janet going to clean?

6. What does Ted want to eat for breakfast?

7. What is Ted going to do with the dirty dishes?

8. What is Ted going to do after they finish cleaning?

B.   Take one out   Read each of these word groups. Take out the word or words that do not belong.

1. rag, cleanser, popcorn, laundry basket

2. sponge, mirror, paper towel, rag

3. dust, sleep, rest, nap

4. vacuum, dust, clean, eat

5. pigsty, nap, mess, dirt

C.   Going to future   Complete each sentence with the correct
going to form of the verb. Follow the example:

Janet _is going to clean_ the bathroom. (clean)

1. Ted _____ a nap. (take)

2. Ted and Janet _____ the apartment. (clean)

3. I _____ you today. (help)

4. He _____ the furniture. (dust)

5. We _____ the laundry together. (do)

6. You _____ very tired after cleaning. (be)

7. Ted _____ cold pizza for breakfast. (eat)

8. Janet _____ the bedroom to wake up her husband.
   (vacuum)

9. I _____ you tomorrow. (call)

10. You and I _____ our work today. (finish)

D. **Want to/would like to**   Change each sentence from **want to** to **would like to.** Use the contraction. Follow the example:

I want to dust the furniture.

I'd like to dust the furniture.

1. She wants to wake him up.

2. I want to clean the bathroom.

3. He wants to sleep some more.

4. They want to finish it today.

5. You want to take a nap.

6. We want to vacuum the apartment.

7. They want to finish cleaning.

8. I want to clean this pigsty.

9. She wants to dust the furniture.

10. We want to take a break.

E.   What do you think?   You are cleaning your house. Decide which items you're going to use for each of the jobs. Write the letter of the correct answer on the line.

a. a sponge and cleanser

b. a rag and furniture polish

c. the vacuum cleaner

d. paper towels and glass cleaner

e. detergent

_____ 1. You need to do your laundry.

_____ 2. You can't see your face in the bathroom mirror.

_____ 3. You'd like to dust the bookcase and the coffee table.

_____ 4. Look at your dirty carpet!

_____ 5. You are going to clean the bathtub.

_____ 6. You are going to clean the kitchen window.

_____ 7. Your kitchen is a pigsty! Wash the dishes.

_____ 8. You'd like to dust the dresser in your bedroom.

_____ 9. How about the dirty rug by the front door?

_____ 10. Now your dishes are clean and dry. How about that messy kitchen sink?

F. Practice these exchanges with a partner. Give short answers to the questions. Use these short answers:

Yes, I would.	No, I wouldn't.
Yes, I do.	No, I don't.
Yes, he/she does.	No, he/she doesn't.
Yes, they do.	No, they don't.

1. **A:** Would you like to help me clean the house?

   B: Yes, ——————— .

2. **A:** Do you have the furniture polish?

   B: No, ——————— .

3. **A:** Does Janet have any more sick time?

   B: No, ——————— .

4. **A:** Would you like to take a nap?

   B: Yes, ——————— .

5. **A:** Does Janet do the laundry?

   B: Yes, ——————— .

6. **A:** Do you sleep late on Saturday mornings?

   B: Yes, _____ .

7. **A:** Would you like to have cold pizza for breakfast?

   B: No, _____ .

8. **A:** Does Ted vacuum the apartment?

   B: Yes, sometimes _____ .

9. **A:** Does your mother wash windows?

   B: No, _____ .

10. **A:** Do Ted and Janet live in a pigsty?

    B: Yes, sometimes _____ .

CHAPTER 5

Don't Chew on the Right Side

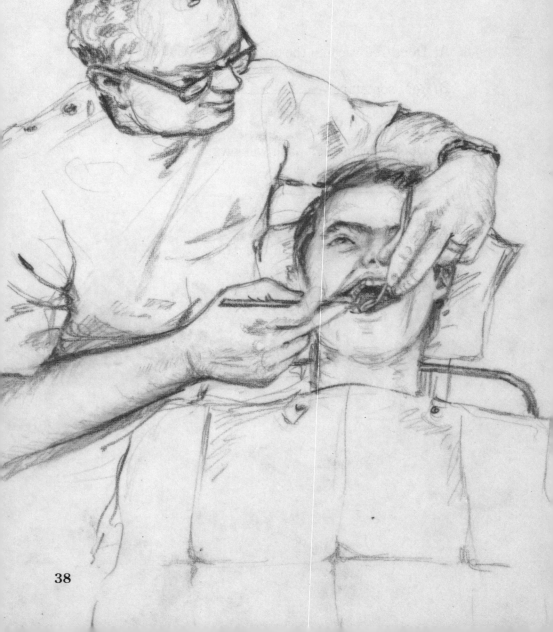

Vocabulary

assistant (n)   helper

cavity (n)   a hole in a tooth

chew (v)   break food inside the mouth

floss (v)   use dental floss to clean between teeth

molar (n)   a tooth in the back of the mouth

rinse (v)   clean with fresh water

sheet (n)   a piece of paper

tartar (n)   a hard, yellow deposit on teeth

twice (adv)   two times

Idioms

Your teeth look **pretty good.**   nice

Keep still.   Don't move. Be quiet.

How's it going?   How are you?

Let's do it.   Let's go ahead. Let's start.

Don't Chew on
the Right Side

Ted doesn't enjoy going to the dentist, but he has an appointment for a check-up and cleaning this afternoon.

Ted hurries into the dentist's office, and signs his name on the sheet. He sits down and waits for the receptionist to call him. He only waits ten minutes.

Ted sits in the dental chair and opens his mouth. The dental assistant cleans his teeth.

"Your teeth look pretty good," she says. "Do you brush and floss a lot?"

Ted tells her that he always brushes his teeth twice a day, and that he uses a fluoride and tartar control toothpaste. He also says that he uses dental floss every night. The assistant finishes cleaning his teeth.

Then Ted goes into a room for X-rays. The assistant says, "I'm going to take some X-rays now. Keep still and don't move. Okay?"

She finishes with the X-rays, and asks Ted to go with her to a different room. She also brings some trays of dental instruments for the dentist.

Ted waits. He's feeling a little nervous now, but he doesn't want the women working in the office to know it.

Soon the dentist comes. Ted would like to leave, but he knows he can't.

DR. PEREZ: Good afternoon, Ted. How's it going?

TED: Fine. How do my X-rays look?

DR. PEREZ: Well, you have two small cavities in your lower right molars. I can fix them today, if you'd like.

TED: Sure. Go ahead. Let's do it.

DR. PEREZ: Okay. I'm going to give you a shot first. I don't want you to feel any pain.

TED: Good. Let's do it.

DR. PEREZ: Open wide.

The dentist gives Ted the shot and waits a couple of minutes.

DR. PEREZ: Do you feel anything now?

TED: No, nothing. Let's go. I'm ready.

DR. PEREZ: All right. Don't move. I'm going to drill the teeth. Then I'm going to fill them. Keep still. Here we go.

The dentist drills Ted's molars and fills his teeth.

DR. PEREZ: There. I'm finished. Here, take some water and rinse your mouth. How do you feel?

TED: I feel fine. I think.

DR. PEREZ: Please don't chew on the right side of your mouth tonight. Wait until tomorrow. Remember to use fluoride toothpaste, a soft toothbrush, and dental floss. I'd like to see you in six months.

TED: Great. Thanks.

Exercises

A.   Answer the questions in complete sentences.

1. For what does Ted have an appointment?

2. Where does Ted hurry?

3. Where does Ted sit and what does he open?

4. What kind of toothpaste does Ted use?

5. What does Ted have in his lower right molars?

6. What is the dentist going to give Ted?

7. What does the dentist do to Ted's teeth?

8. When does the dentist want to see Ted?

B.   True or false   Read each sentence. Write **T** on the line if it is true. Write **F** on the line if it is false.

_____ 1. A molar is a tooth in the front of your mouth.

_____ 2. **Keep still** means **don't move** or **be quiet.**

_____ 3. When you rinse your mouth, you clean your mouth with fresh water.

_____ 4. A dental assistant fills cavities.

_____ 5. Use dental floss to clean between your teeth.

_____ 6. **Twice** means two times.

_____ 7. A soft toothbrush is bad for your teeth.

_____ 8. A cavity is a hole in your tooth.

C.   Spelling   Complete each sentence. Use the correct plural or the correct third person singular present tense form. Follow the example:

His dentist has offices in two ____cities____ .
(city)

1. The dental assistant _____ a tray into the room.
   (carry)

2. The dentist wants two _____ of dental instruments.
   (tray)

3. One of the _____ is a receptionist.   (lady)

4. He doesn't want the _____ working in the office to know that he's nervous.   (woman)

5. She's going to clean his _____ .   (tooth)

6. You have two _____ in your molars.   (cavity)

7. Janet usually _____ the toothpaste.   (buy)

8. She's going to take some _____ .   (X-ray)

9. Ted is late, so he _____ into the dentist's office.
   (hurry)

10. No one _____ going to the dentist.   (enjoy)

D.   Imperative   Give a command for each sentence. Use **please** to be polite. Follow the example:

Ted's not keeping still.

Please keep still.

1. He's not opening wide.

2. She's not using dental floss.

3. You're not brushing with a soft toothbrush.

4. Ted's not getting a dental check-up.

5. Janet's not using tartar control toothpaste.

E.   Imperative   Give a negative command for each sentence. Use **please** to be polite. Follow the example:

> Ted's moving his head.

> **Please don't move your head.**

1. You're using a hard toothbrush.

2. She's forgetting to brush at night.

3. He's eating too much sugar.

4. You're late for your dental appointment.

5. Ted's chewing on the right side of his mouth.

F.   Dialogues   Practice one of these dialogues with a partner. Present it to the class.

Dialogue One

A: May I help you?

B: Yes. I have a dental appointment. My name is _____ .

A: All right, Mr./Ms. _____ . Have a seat.

B: Will it take long?

A: Not very long. I'll call your name in a few minutes.

B: Thank you. I'll read a magazine.

Dialogue Two

A: Good afternoon, _____ . How's it going?

B: Fine. How do my X-rays look?

A: You have two cavities in your lower right molars.

B: Can you fix them today?

A: Yes. I'm going to give you a shot first.

B: Good. I don't want to feel any pain.

Dialogue Three

A: Open wide now, Mr./Ms. _____ . Please don't move.

B: What are you going to do? Is it going to hurt?

A: No. I'm just going to clean your teeth.

B: What about X-rays? I think I have a cavity.

A: We're going to take X-rays in a few minutes.

B: All right. Let's do it. I'm ready.

Dialogue Four

A: Do you floss your teeth every day?

B: Yes, I do. And I brush twice a day.

A: Your teeth look pretty good.

B: I brush with a tartar control toothpaste.

A: Good. But you need to use a soft toothbrush.

B: Really? Okay. I'm going to buy one today.

CHAPTER 6

The Money Saver

Vocabulary

bargain (n)   a good price, a special

coupon (n)   a small piece of paper that gives a discount

discount (n)   less money, money off

double (n)   two times

grocery shopping (n)   buying things at the supermarket

item (n)   one thing, one product

kind (n)   type, category

remind (v)   tell somebody to remember

veggies (n)   vegetables

Idioms

I'm **tired of** chicken.   bored with

We can **check it out** at the store.   look at it, examine it

I don't care.   It isn't important to me.

Pick out a couple of good ones.   choose

No way.   It's impossible.

The Money Saver

Ted and Janet usually do their supermarket shopping early Friday evening. That way they can do the shopping together. Janet makes the shopping list. Ted usually reminds her to put certain items on the list, like zucchini, avocados, peanuts and beer.

Janet saves coupons. There's a supermarket in town that has a lot of bargains and gives double the discount on coupons. Janet likes to do her grocery shopping there.

This week she has coupons for 45¢ off coffee, 20¢ off lunchmeat, 15¢ off paper towels, and 30¢ off butter. She has many more coupons. Janet knows that the supermarket is going to double these discounts.

Janet's checking her shopping list now. She's getting ready for the weekly grocery shopping. She wants to be sure that she has everything on the list.

"Honey," she says to her husband. "Do we need anything else from the grocery store? I'm checking this week's list."

Ted answers, "We need beer."

"I have that," she says.

"How about some pork this time? I'm tired of chicken."

"Okay," answers Janet. "The store is having a special on pork. No problem. Anything else, honey?"

"Well, I'd like some peanuts. Do you think they're too expensive?"

"I don't know," she says. "We can check it out at the store."

Ted and Janet are now in the supermarket. They're buying the items they need.

JANET: I have a coupon for this butter. Let's get it.

TED: Okay. Are we going to buy that white cheese again?

JANET: Sure. Why not?

TED: I really don't like it. How about this? Cheddar.

JANET: I don't care. I'm not eating cheese anymore. I think it has too much fat.

TED: But you're eating meat, right? Look at these great bargains on steak and lamb.

JANET: Well, let's get two steaks. We can barbecue tonight. Pick out a couple of good ones, honey. No fat.

TED: How about a nice big salad with the steaks? Let's check out the fresh veggies.

JANET: Okay. I'd like to have cucumber and tomato in my salad.

TED: Hey, bananas! I love bananas! Let's get some.

JANET: At 75¢ a pound? No way, Ted!

TED: Janet, I like bananas. I don't care about the price. I'm going to get some.

JANET: All right. But we're not going to buy any of these strawberries or those grapes. They're really too expensive.

TED: Okay, honey. You're the money saver of the family.

Exercises

A. Answer the questions in complete sentences.

1. When do Ted and Janet usually do their supermarket shopping?

2. What does Janet save?

3. What does the supermarket in their town give?

4. What is Ted tired of?

5. What does Janet have for the butter?

6. What cheese doesn't Ted like?

7. What are the great bargains on?

8. Who is the money saver of the family?

B. **Multiple choice**   Choose **a**, **b** or **c** as the correct answer.

1. Janet says, "Pick out two good steaks." This means _____ .

   a. look at two good steaks

   b. choose two good steaks

   c. pay for two good steaks

2. Ted says, "I'm tired of chicken." This means _____ .

   a. Ted loves chicken

   b. Ted wants to buy chicken

   c. Ted doesn't want to buy chicken

3. Janet doesn't want to pay 75¢ a pound for bananas. She tells her husband, _____

    a. "No way."

    b. "All right."

    c. "I don't care."

4. Ted and Janet are going to look at the price of peanuts. They're going to _____ .

    a. pick it out

    b. use a coupon

    c. check it out

5. Ted usually reminds Janet to put certain items on the list. This means that Ted _____ .

    a. buys groceries with Janet

    b. tells Janet what he wants

    c. picks out veggies with Janet

6. A bargain is a _____ .

    a. good price

    b. coupon

    c. item

7. Ted says, "I don't care about the price." This means _____ .

    a. Ted doesn't like the price

    b. Ted thinks it's too expensive

    c. the price isn't important to Ted

8. The supermarket gives double the discount on coupons. This means it _____ .

    a. gives two times the money off a coupon

    b. always has specials

    c. is always cheap

C.   Demonstratives   Complete each sentence with the correct demonstrative: **this, that, these,** or **those.**

1. I don't like _____ cheese. (over there)

2. Let's buy some of _____ veggies. (right here)

3. Do you want any of _____ items? (over there)

4. Would you like to buy _____ cleanser? (over there)

5. Are you going to use _____ coupon? (right here)

6. She has a coupon for _____ butter. (right here)

7. There's a great bargain on _____ steaks. (right here)

8. Let's check out _____ peanuts. (over there)

9. The store doesn't have a special on _____ item. (over there)

10. They do their shopping at _____ store. (over there)

D.   Mixed tenses   Complete each sentence with the present, present continuous, or **going to** form of the verb. Follow the example:

Ted and Janet __are going to look__ for bargains next Friday evening. (look)

1. Janet ＿＿＿＿＿＿ her shopping list now. (check)

2. They ＿＿＿＿＿＿ shopping every Friday evening. (go)

3. I ＿＿＿＿＿＿ some bananas tomorrow. (buy)

4. Janet ＿＿＿＿＿＿ ready right now. (get)

5. We always ＿＿＿＿＿＿ out good bargains. (pick)

6. Ted usually ＿＿＿＿＿＿ Janet to put certain items on the list. (remind)

7. Later they ＿＿＿＿＿＿ steaks and salad. (have)

8. The supermarket ＿＿＿＿＿＿ double the discount on coupons. (give)

9. You and I usually ＿＿＿＿＿＿ cheese. (buy)

10. Janet ＿＿＿＿＿＿ coupons every week. (save)

E. Coupons   Read each coupon. Match the information with the correct coupon. Write the letter of the correct answer on the line.

a.

> # SAVE 25¢
>
> # FEEL-FRESH SOAP
>
> ## Stay fresh all day
>
> Expires 3/31/99   Any size
>
> **SAVE 25¢**

b.

> ## SAVE 50¢
> # PITT'S ORANGE JUICE
>
> Good on gallon size only
>
> No expiration date

c.

> # 30¢ OFF MOM'S COOKIES
>
> when you buy two
> 12 oz. boxes
>
> ## GOOD ON CHOCOLATE CHIP ONLY
>
> Expires 9/15/98

_____ 1. You can use this coupon anytime.

_____ 2. You must buy two.

_____ 3. It expires in March.

_____ 4. If the price is $1.98, you pay only $1.68 with this coupon.

_____ 5. It's not good for the quart size.

_____ 6. It's good for the small or the large size.

———— 7. If the supermarket gives you double the discount on coupons, you save $1.00.

———— 8. This coupon is not good for oatmeal and raisin cookies.

F. Ask your partner Practice asking and answering questions with a partner. Read these instructions and ask the correct questions. Your partner must answer in complete sentences. Then, have your partner ask you the questions.

1. Ask when he or she goes grocery shopping. (When do you . . . ?)

2. Ask what he or she buys. (What do you . . . ?)

3. Ask if he or she saves coupons. (Do you . . . ?)

4. Ask if he or she is going to buy steak next week. (Are you . . . ?)

5. Ask if he or she is going to make a shopping list. (Are you . . . ?)

6. Ask if the supermarket is going to give double discounts. (Is the supermarket . . . ?)

7. Ask if he or she is shopping right now. (Are you . . . ?)

8. Ask if he or she is getting ready for shopping now. (Are you . . . ?)

9. Ask if he or she likes to go shopping. (Do you . . . ?)

10. Ask what supermarket he or she goes to. (What supermarket do you . . . ?)

CHAPTER 7

One More Dollar

Vocabulary

bagger (n)　　supermarket worker who puts groceries in bags

cart (n)　　a large basket on wheels

check-cashing card (n)　　a card that allows a customer to write a check

checker (n)　　supermarket cashier

check-out (n)　　the place where shoppers pay for groceries

customer (n)　　shopper

expired (adj)　　old, out-of-date

express lane (n)　　a check-out that takes cash only from shoppers with fewer than twelve items

total (n)　　the amount of all the groceries plus tax

Idioms

What's the matter?　　What's wrong?

There's something wrong.　　There's a problem.

I have **so many** coupons.　　very many

Throw the expired coupons **away**.　　put in the trash

One More Dollar

Ted and Janet are now at the supermarket check-out. The supermarket is busy tonight, and there are many people standing in line. Ted and Janet are going to pay cash for their groceries, but they can't go to the express lane because their basket is full. There are more than twelve items in their cart, so they're standing in the regular lane. They're waiting and waiting.

"There are so many people in this line. What's taking so long?" Ted asks. He's getting upset.

"I think there's a problem. That customer wants to write a check, but she doesn't have a check-cashing card."

"This supermarket is always slow. And there's always a problem. Why do we shop here?" Ted asks.

"Double coupons," Janet answers. "And good bargains."

"Money! Money! Money!" Ted says.

Now Ted and Janet are next. The checker is looking at the jar of peanuts. She doesn't see a price on the jar.

"Excuse me," she says. "Do you know the cost of these?"

Ted and Janet don't know how much they are.

"Well, I need to send the bagger to check it out. Ron," she calls, "please find the price of these peanuts."

"Not again!" says Ted. "There's always a problem at this market!"

"Sh! She'll hear you!" says Janet.

Now the checker is finished. She tells Ted and Janet the total.

CHECKER: That's $74.53.

JANET: Oh, wait! I have so many coupons. Here.

CHECKER: Okay. Give me a minute and I . . . Oh-oh.

TED: What's the matter? Is there something wrong? A problem?

CHECKER: Yes, there is. Some of your coupons are expired.

JANET: Really? How many old coupons are there?

CHECKER: There are four expired coupons, but these are good.

TED: Well, throw the expired ones away.

CHECKER: Now your total is $68.17.

Janet gives the checker four twenty-dollar bills.

CHECKER: Out of $80.00.

The checker gives Janet three pennies, a nickel, three quarters, and a ten-dollar bill.

CHECKER: Thank you. Have a nice day.

JANET: Wait a minute. This isn't right. I need a dollar.

CHECKER: Are you sure? Count it again.

JANET: I know I'm right. Look. The total is $68.17. Three pennies make 20¢. A nickel makes 25¢. Three quarters make $69.00. Now there's a ten-dollar bill. That makes $79.00, not $80.00. I need a dollar.

CHECKER: You're right. I'm so sorry. Here you are.

JANET: That's okay. Bye.

TED: Wow! What a supermarket!

JANET: No problem, honey. I always count my change.

Exercises

A.   Answer the questions in complete sentences.

1. Where are Ted and Janet?

2. Why can't they go to the express lane?

3. A customer wants to write a check. What's the problem?

4. Who needs to check the price of the peanuts?

5. Why is Ted upset?

6. How many expired coupons are there?

7. Something's wrong with the change. What does Janet need?

8. What does Janet always count?

B.   **True or false**   Read each sentence. Write **T** on the line if the sentence is true. Write **F** on the line if the sentence is false.

_____ 1. A bagger puts groceries into bags.

_____ 2. A shopper can have twenty items at the express lane.

———— 3. The total is the price of one item.

———— 4. A customer sells items.

———— 5. An expired coupon is good.

———— 6. The supermarket checker works at the check-out.

———— 7. If there's something wrong, there's a problem.

———— 8. If you throw something away, you put it in the trash.

———— 9. A shopping cart is a basket on wheels.

———— 10. A check-cashing card is a coupon.

C.   There is/There are   Complete each sentence with singular **there is** or plural **there are**. Follow the example:

_____There are_____ many coupons for their groceries.

1. __there are__ so many people standing in line.

2. _____is___ always a problem at this supermarket.

3. _____are more than twelve items in their cart.

4. I think ____there is___ something wrong.

5. ___there are__ four twenty-dollar bills here.

6. ___there are__ so many bargains at this market.

7. ___there is___ no price on the peanuts.

8. ___there are__ two express lanes at this place.

9. _____ a bagger that checks out the prices.

10. _____ some shopping carts over there.

D.   There is/There are   Change each sentence to a question. Follow the example:

> There are twelve items in their basket.

> **Are there twelve items in their basket?**

1. There's a problem.

2. There are four expired coupons.

3. There's an express lane.

4. There are many people in line.

5. There's a customer writing a check.

E.   Contractions   Change each sentence or question by using a contraction. Follow the example:

> This is not right.

> **This isn't right.**

1. What is the price of these?

2. There is not a special on beef.

3. He is checking the price.

4. That is okay.

5. What is the matter?

6. I know I am right.

7. Ted and Janet do not know the price of the peanuts.

8. They are going to pay cash.

9. Ted is getting upset.

10. Sh! She will hear you!

F.   Dialogues   Practice giving and receiving change with a partner. Remember to count the change. Follow the example:

> **A:** The total is $16.82.
>
> **B:** Here's a twenty.
>
> **A:** Out of $20.00. (Give three pennies, a nickel, a dime and three dollars. Count it.) $16.82, 85¢, 90¢, $17.00, $18.00, $19.00 and $20.00. Thank you and have a nice day.
>
> **B:** Thank you. Bye.

1.   **A:** The total is $6.24.

> **B:** (Give a twenty to the checker.) Here you are.
>
> **A:** Do you have a quarter?
>
> **B:** I'm sorry. I don't.

A: Okay. (Give a penny, three quarters, three ones, and a

ten-dollar bill. Count it.) $6.24, _____ .

B: Thank you.

2.   **A:** That's $4.16.

B: I only have a ten.

A: Okay. Out of ten. (Give four pennies, a nickel, three

quarters, and a five-dollar bill. Count it.)

$4.16, _____ .

3.   **A:** Here's your change. Have a nice day.

B: Wait a minute. I need one more dollar.

A: Are you sure? Count it again.

B: The total is $26.42. Out of $30.00. (Count three

pennies, a nickel, two quarters and two dollars.)

$26.42, _____ . That's $29.00, not $30.00.

A: I'm sorry. Here you are. (Give a dollar.)

4.   **A:** The total is $3.01. Do you have a penny?

   B: No, I'm sorry. I don't.

   A: Okay. Out of $5.00. (Give four pennies, two dimes, three quarters, and a dollar. Count it.)

   $3.01, _____ .

   B: Thank you. Bye.

   A: Have a nice day.

5.   **A:** That's $21.25.

   B: Here's a twenty and a five.

   A: Here's your change. (Give three quarters and three dollars. Count it.)

   $21.25, _____ .

   B: Thanks.

CHAPTER 8

She's Going to Be Fifty

Vocabulary

box (n) a container for sending things in the mail

fantastic (adj) terrific, great

mind (n) brain, memory

print (adj) covered with a design, like flowers

scarf (n) a piece of clothing that a person wears around his or her neck

striped (adj) covered with lines

wool (n) material from sheep hair

Idioms

Are you kidding? Are you joking?

I'll **make sure** we still have them. be sure

They **go together**. match, look nice together

Charge it, please. pay for it by credit card

I'll **be back** for your next sale. return

She's Going to Be Fifty

There was something important on Janet's mind.

"What is it? What is it?" she thinks aloud. "I need to remember something."

"Ted," she calls, "what's happening this Sunday? Do you remember? I'm sure there's something important to remember."

Ted puts down his newspaper and thinks.

"Well," he says, "there's a fantastic football game on TV at 1:00. Is that it?" Ted is kidding.

"Oh, Ted! I'm not joking. Think!"

Ted and Janet are very quiet. They are both thinking of the important thing that's going to happen next Sunday. Then Ted remembers.

"Oh, my gosh! I remember now. It's my mother's birthday! She'll be fifty years old next Sunday."

"That's right. I remember, too," Janet says. "There was a letter from your father. He's going to give her a big party."

Ted's parents live in Chicago. Ted and Janet aren't going to the birthday party.

Now they're thinking of a present to buy for his mother. They need to send it to Chicago.

"There were some sales at the department stores," Janet says.

"Sales! Are you kidding? Janet, please don't think about money! It's my mother's birthday. She's going to be fifty!"

Janet says she's sorry. "I'll be happy to go shopping tomorrow and buy something expensive," she says.

"Thanks, honey," Ted answers. "But not too expensive."

Janet is at a department store. A salesclerk is helping her.

CLERK: How about this pink print blouse? It's only $29.95 on sale.

JANET: I'm not sure. Do you have anything more expensive? It's for my mother-in-law.

CLERK: I understand. There were some very nice wool sweaters. I'll make sure we still have them.

The clerk leaves. Janet looks at some dresses. The clerk returns.

CLERK: I'm very sorry. We don't have those sweaters now. But how about these terrific striped dresses. Very expensive!

JANET: I don't know. What does a mother-in-law want?

CLERK: She wants her son back. Ha-ha. I'm joking. How about these terrific scarves?

JANET: They're very pretty. How much is this purple scarf?

CLERK: It's $14.95. It looks fantastic with that pink print blouse.

JANET: You're right. They go together. I think she'll be very happy with a blouse and a scarf. Do you have boxes? I need a box. I need to send it to Chicago.

CLERK: Yes, we do. Cash or charge?

JANET: Charge, please.

CLERK: Anything else?

JANET: Not today. I'll be back for your next sale.

Exercises

A.   Answer the questions in complete sentences.

1. What was there on Janet's mind?

2. What is there on TV at 1:00 this Sunday?

3. How old will Ted's mother be next Sunday?

4. What are they thinking of now?

5. What will Janet be happy to do tomorrow?

6. How much is the pink print blouse?

7. Why does Janet need a box?

8. How does Janet pay for the gift?

B.   Spelling es/ves   Complete each sentence with the correct spelling of the word. Add **es** or change **f / fe** to **ves**. Follow the example:

> The sweaters are on the _____shelves_____ .
> (shelf)

1. I like these pink print _____ . (dress)

2. The _____ are going shopping. (wife)

3. Ted always _____ Janet hello and good-bye.
   (kiss)

4. The purple scarf _____ the pink blouse.
   (match)

5. _____ are full of people on Sunday morning.
   (church)

6. These _____ are on sale. (scarf)

7. Do you have any _____ ? (box)

8. The _____ are in the kitchen. (knife)

C.   Matching   Find the sentence in column B that has the same meaning as the sentence in column A. Write the letter of the correct answer on the line.

A	**B**
_____ 1. I'm kidding.	a. It's terrific.
_____ 2. It's fantastic.	b. There were some dresses with lines.
_____ 3. These sweaters are wool.	c. I'll return.
_____ 4. There were some striped dresses.	d. The flowered dresses cost a lot.
_____ 5. The purple scarf and the pink blouse go together.	e. Wear it around your neck.
_____ 6. I'll be back.	f. I'm joking.
_____ 7. It's a scarf.	g. They match.
_____ 8. The print dresses are expensive.	h. These sweaters come from sheep hair.

D.   There was/there were   Complete each sentence with singular **there was** or plural **there were**. Follow the example:

    <u>There were</u>   many dresses on sale.

1. _____ a letter from Ted's father.

2. _____ some striped dresses in the store.

3. _____ a purple scarf for $14.95.

4. _____ some very nice wool sweaters.

5. _____ something important on her mind.

6. _____ a sale at that store.

7. _____ a fantastic football game on TV.

8. _____ many people at the department store.

E.   Talking with a salesclerk   Practice this dialogue with a partner. Make questions or sentences by putting the words in the correct order. Follow the example:

    blouse / How / this / print / about?   How about this print blouse?

    CLERK: you / I / help / May?

    CUSTOMER: see / want / something / I / mother-in-law / to / for / my.

    CLERK: on / sweaters / nice / sale / There / some / very / are.

    CUSTOMER: anything / have / more / Do / expensive / you?

CLERK: about / terrific / this / How / dress / purple?

CUSTOMER: it / cost / much / does / How?

CLERK: only / $89.98 / It's.

CUSTOMER: happy / I / it / she'll / think / be / very / with.

CLERK: charge / want / you / it / Do / to?

CUSTOMER: pay / I'll / cash.

F. Ask your partner   Practice asking and answering questions with a partner. Read these instructions and ask the correct questions. Your partner must answer in complete sentences. Then, have your partner ask you the questions.

1. Ask what's happening this Sunday. (What's . . . ?)

2. Ask if there's going to be a party at his or her house. (Is there . . . ?)

3. Ask how old his or her mother will be. (How old will . . . ?)

4. Ask if he or she is going shopping tomorrow. (Are you . . . ?)

5. Ask if he or she needs to remember something important. (Do you . . . ?)

6. Ask if he or she likes the purple scarf. (Do you . . . ?)

7. Ask if he or she needs to send a box to Chicago. (Do you . . . ?)

8. Ask if he or she wants to charge it. (Do you . . . ?)

CHAPTER 9

First Class to Chicago

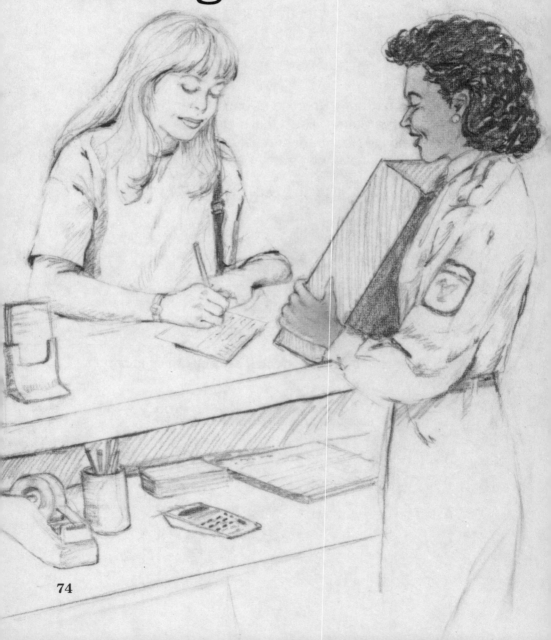

Vocabulary

drawer (n)   the part of a dresser that pulls out

dresser (n)   bedroom furniture for clothes

first class (n)   fast mail

insure (v)   buy insurance

parcel (n)   package

parcel post (n)   inexpensive mail for packages

weigh (v)   find the weight of something

Idioms

Ted and Janet were **running late.**   late, going to be late

You really should **take care of** your things.   be careful with

I'm **in a hurry.**   hurrying, running late

No problem.   There's no trouble. It's okay.

My pleasure.   I'm happy to help you.

First Class to Chicago

It was early the next morning, and Ted and Janet were running late.

"Janet!" says Ted. "Where are my brown socks? I can't find them."

Janet says that his brown socks are in his top drawer.

"Janet!" calls Ted again. "Where's my belt? Would you help me, honey? I'm late."

Janet gives the belt to him. "Here, Ted," Janet says. "You really should take care of your things."

Ted thanks Janet. Then he asks, "Hon, where are my brown shoes? They were under the bed yesterday. Will you help me? I'm in a hurry."

This time Janet won't help him. "Ted," she answers, "I don't know where your shoes are. I don't wear them!" Janet was in a hurry, too.

Then Ted sees his mother's birthday gift. It's sitting on Janet's dresser. The gift must arrive in Chicago by Saturday, so they must mail the package today.

"Janet! Janet!" Ted calls. "Would you go to the post office this afternoon and mail Mom's gift?"

"Oh! The gift! That's right!" Janet says. "Sure, honey. I'll go to the post office this afternoon. No problem."

It's afternoon now. Janet's at the post office.

CLERK: Good afternoon. May I help you?

JANET: Yes. I'd like to send this package to Chicago. Parcel post, please.

CLERK: Parcel post to Chicago may take ten days. Is that okay?

JANET: Ten days! Oh, no! That will be too late. This is for my mother-in-law's birthday. Can I send it first class?

CLERK: Sure, but it's more expensive.

JANET: I don't care. How much is it?

CLERK: The parcel weighs three pounds. That's $5.81.

JANET: How long will it take to arrive? This package can't be late.

CLERK: First class to Chicago will take three days.

JANET: That's good. Should I insure it?

CLERK: It's a good idea. Insurance is cheap.

JANET: Well, the cost of this present is about $50.00.

CLERK: $50.00? That's $1.10 for insurance. Please fill out this form. You get a copy.

JANET: What happens if the parcel gets lost?

CLERK: If something happens to the package, report it to the post office.

JANET: Okay. Thanks for your help.

CLERK: Sure. My pleasure. I was happy to help.

Exercises

A. Answer the questions in complete sentences.

1. Where are Ted's brown socks?

2. Where were Ted's shoes yesterday?

3. What does Ted see on Janet's dresser?

4. Where will Janet go this afternoon?

5. How long may parcel post to Chicago take?

6. How much does the parcel weigh?

7. Should Janet insure the package?

8. How much is the insurance?

B. Take one out Read each of these word groups. Take out the word or words that do not belong.

1. first class, parcel post, dresser, insurance

2. present, problem, gift, package

3. drawer, send, mail, insure

4. may, should, would, don't

5. all right, fill out, no problem, okay

6. You're welcome, My pleasure, I don't care, Thank you

C. To be Complete each sentence with the correct present, past or future tense of **to be**. Follow the example:

> Ted and Janet _____were_____ late for work yesterday.

1. I _____ at the post office tomorrow afternoon.

2. Ted _____ in a hurry early this morning.

3. Janet _____ usually in a hurry in the morning.

4. Her ankle _____ swollen last week.

5. The package _____ in Chicago next Saturday.

6. We _____ always late on Mondays.

7. The Parkers _____ running late yesterday morning.

8. I _____ never late for school.

9. The sick clerk _____ back at the post office next week.

10. His shoes _____ under the bed yesterday.

D. Short story Complete the sentences with a modal. Use **should, must, will, would, can,** or **may.**

Ted asks Janet, "Where are my socks? I can't find them."

Janet says, "I don't know. You <u>should</u> really take care of your
(1)

things, Ted."

Then Ted sees his mother's birthday gift on Janet's dresser. He

asks, "Janet ———— you take it to the post office this afternoon? It
(2)

———— arrive in Chicago by Saturday."
(3)

At the post office, Janet says to the clerk, "I ———— like to
(4)

send this package to Chicago. ———— I send it parcel post?"
(5)

The clerk says, "Parcel post to Chicago ———— take ten days.
(6)

First class ———— take three days. ———— you like first class?"
(7)   (8)

Janet says, "Yes, I ————. ———— I insure it?"
(9)   (10)

The clerk tells her that it's a good idea.

E.   Parcel service   Read these parcel service prices and
answer the questions.

Bingman Parcel Service

Weight	Zone 1	Zone 2	Zone 3
Under 1 lb.	$1.25	$1.85	$2.45
Over 1 lb. to 3 lbs.	$1.58	$2.12	$2.70
Over 3 lbs. to 6 lbs.	$1.85	$2.40	$2.98
Over 6 lbs. to 10 lbs.	$2.06	$2.60	$3.20
Over 10 lbs. to 15 lbs.	$2.31	$2.85	$3.45

1. How much will a six-pound parcel to Zone 2 cost?

   ————————

2. Which shipping zone costs the most? ————

3. If Janet sends a two-pound package to Zone 1, and a nine-pound package to Zone 3, how much will she pay? _____

4. How much will Janet pay to send a twelve-pound parcel to Zone 2? _____ How much will she pay to send it to Zone 3? _____

5. Janet pays $2.06 to send a package to Zone 1. How much does the package weigh? _____

6. Janet pays $1.85 for a ten-ounce parcel. What zone is it going to? _____

F. Dialogues   Practice one of these dialogues with a partner. Present it to the class.

Dialogue One

A: Afternoon. May I help you?

B: Yes. I'd like to send this parcel to Chicago.

A: Would you like parcel post or first class?

B: First class, please. Parcel post is too slow.

A: The package weighs five pounds. That's $5.81.

B: Okay. The package must be there by Saturday.

Dialogue Two

A: How long will it take to arrive?

B: First class to Chicago will take three days.

A: That's good. Should I insure it?

B: It's a good idea. Insurance is cheap.

A: Well, the cost of this present is about $50.00.

B: $50.00? That's $1.10 for insurance.

Dialogue Three

A: Where are my brown socks? I can't find them.

B: They're in your top drawer.

A: Where's my belt? Would you help me? I'm in a hurry.

B: Here it is. You really should take care of your things.

A: Oh-oh! My mother's gift! Can you mail it today?

B: No problem. I'll go to the post office this afternoon.

Dialogue Four

A: I'd like to send this package parcel post.

B: Parcel post to Chicago may take ten days.

A: Ten days! Oh, no. That will be too late.

B: Would you like to send it first class?

A: Yes, and I'd like to insure it for $50.00.

B: First class with insurance is $6.91.

A: Okay. Thanks for your help.

B: Sure. My pleasure.

CHAPTER 10

Dial "9" First

Vocabulary

area code (n)   a number that shows a certain calling area

asleep (adj)   sleeping

collect call (n)   a phone call for which the person receiving the call pays

dial (v)   use the numbers to make a phone call

difference (n)   a different amount

employee (n)   worker

together (adv)   two or more people in one place

Idioms

Will you **accept the charges**?   say that you'll pay for a collect call

Where should I **pick** you **up**?   drive to a place and get a person

Will they **need a ride**?   need someone to drive a person to a place

I **miss you**.   feel sad or homesick about a person

Dial "9" First

Ted is in Dallas, Texas, for a couple of days. It's a business trip. He's there with a lot of people from his company. There are many employees from many companies at the hotel. Janet's not on the business trip with Ted. She's at home.

Each morning, Ted meets some of the employees that he knows from work. They have breakfast together. Then they go to an important meeting. After the morning meeting, the employees usually have lunch together. There are more meetings in the afternoon.

Last night there was a big party at the hotel for all of the visiting employees. Ted was at the party. It was a very late party, so this morning Ted doesn't want to go downstairs for breakfast. He wants to stay in bed some more. He's reading the newspaper now. He has a lot of time before the first big meeting.

After he reads the paper, Ted thinks, "Gee, I'd like to talk to Janet. I miss her. Maybe I'll call her collect."

Ted picks up the phone and dials "9" first so he can call out of the hotel. He dials "0" and the area code for San Diego next. Then he dials his home phone number. An operator answers.

OPERATOR: Operator.

TED: Yes, I'd like to make this a collect call.

OPERATOR: What is your name, please?

TED: My name's Ted.

OPERATOR: Thank you. One moment.

The operator dials their number in California. The telephone rings. Janet answers the phone. She's very tired because she was asleep.

JANET: Helloooo?

OPERATOR: I have a collect call for anyone from Ted. Will you accept the charges?

JANET: Whooo? Ted? Ted who? Oh! Yes, I will.

OPERATOR: Thank you. Go ahead, please.

TED: Hello, Janet? Hi, honey. How are you?

JANET: Hi, hon. What are you doing? Why are you calling me?

TED: I'm calling you because I miss you. What's the matter? Why are you so tired? Were you asleep?

JANET: Yes, I was.

TED: I'm sorry, baby. What time is it there?

JANET: It's only 5:00. There's a two-hour difference between Dallas and San Diego, you know.

TED: Sorry, hon. Remember, I'll be home tomorrow night. Can you pick me up at the airport?

JANET: Sure. No problem. When do you arrive?

TED: At 8:45 P.M.

JANET: Where should I pick you up?

TED: I'm flying Tails Up Airlines.

JANET: How many people will be with you? Will they need a ride?

TED: There will be a lot of employees on the plane, but only Mack Mackay will need a ride.

JANET: Okay. We can drive him home.

TED: Super. Janet? I miss you.

JANET: I miss you, too, honey. See you tomorrow night.

TED: Okay, baby. Bye. Go back to sleep.

Exercises

A.   Answer the questions in complete sentences.

1. Where is Ted?

2. Whom does he meet each morning?

3. What was there at the hotel last night?

4. Why does Ted want to talk to Janet?

5. First Ted dials "9." What does he dial next?

6. What kind of call does Ted make?

7. Why is Janet so tired?

8. What time is it in San Diego? And in Dallas?

B. **Multiple choice**   Choose **a**, **b**, or **c** as the correct answer.

1. An employee _____ .

    a. lives at a hotel

    b. works for a company

    c. makes collect calls

2. If you need a ride home, you need _____ .

    a. someone to take you home

    b. someone to call you at home

    c. to go on a business trip

3. Ted says, "I miss you, Janet." This means _____ .

    a. he'll be home tomorrow night

    b. he wants to see Janet

    c. Janet will accept the charges

4. There's a two-hour difference between Dallas and San Diego. This means _____ .

    a. you must make a collect call from Dallas

    b. Dallas is in Texas

    c. if it's 7:00 in Dallas, it is 5:00 in San Diego

5. If you want to call a different state collect, you must dial _____ .

    a. the number

    b. the area code and the number

    c. "0" and the area code and the number

6. Ted's dialing 0–555–480–1222. The area code is ———— .

   a. 555

   b. 480

   c. 0

7. Some of the employees eat lunch together. This means that they ———— .

   a. eat at the hotel

   b. meet for lunch

   c. have lunch after the morning meeting

8. Janet's going to pick Ted up at the airport. She's going to ———— .

   a. call him collect at the airport

   b. give him a ride home from the airport

   c. go on a business trip with him

C.   Word order   Make a sentence or a question by putting the words in the correct order.

1. dials / call / so / "9" / He / hotel / out / the / of / he / can.

2. you / tired / Why / so / are?

3. plane / on / a / employees / lot / There / be / of / will / the.

4. up / Where / you / I / pick / should?

5. because / you / I'm / miss / calling / you / I.

D.   Matching   Read the telephone call that each person makes in **A**. Match it with the sentence from **B** that means the same. Write the letter of the correct answer on the line.

A   **B**

_____ 1. Nick dials "9" first.   a. This person has an
                                                 emergency.

_____ 2. Sue dials 911.   b. This person is dialing a
                                                 no-charge number.

_____ 3. Jack dials "0" first.   c. This person has a
                                                 wrong number.

_____ 4. Ben dials "1-800"   d. This person is in a
            first.   hotel or office.

_____ 5. Nancy dials "1-area   e. This person needs
            code" first.   directory assistance.
                                                 (Information)

_____ 6. Ron dials the number.   f. This person is dialing
            He hangs up and dials   long distance direct.
            again.

_____ 7. Keith dials 411.   g. This person needs the
                                                 operator's help.

E.   Short story   Complete the sentences with the correct forms of the verbs.

Ted __is__ in Dallas, Texas now. He _____ there with a lot
    (1) be   (2) be

of people from his company. There _____ many employees from
                                      (3) be

many companies at the hotel. Every morning, Ted _____ some
                                                  (4) meet

of the employees that he knows from work. They _____
                                                 (5) have

breakfast together.

Last night there _____ a big party for all of the visiting
                  (6) be

employees. It _____ a late party, so this morning Ted
               (7) be

_____ to go downstairs.
(8) not/want

He _____ now, but he _____ Janet. Ted _____ up the
    (9) read   (10) miss   (11) pick

telephone to make a collect call. He _____ "0" and says,
                                      (12) dial

"I _____ to make a collect call." The operator _____ him.
   (13) like   (14) help

F. Practice making a long distance collect call with partners.

A: Operator.

B: Yes, operator. I'd like to make a _____ .

A: What is _____ ?

B: My _____ .

A: One moment, please. I'm ringing the number.

The phone rings in the other city.

C: Hello?

A: I have a collect call for anyone from _____ . Will you accept the charges?

C: Yes, I will.

A: Thank you. Go ahead, please.

B: Hi, _____ . How are you? What are you doing?

C: I'm fine. I'm _____ right now.

B: Can you pick me up _____ ?

C: Sure. No problem. When do _____ ?

B: I arrive _____ .

C: Okay. See you _____ . Bye.

B: Bye.

CHAPTER 11

Passengers Only at This Point

Passengers Only At This Point

Vocabulary

announcement (n)   important information that people need to hear

arrival (n)   the landing of a plane

delayed (adj)   late because of a problem

flight (n)   a trip on a plane

gate (n)   the place where the plane arrives at the airport

order (v)   ask for something to eat or drink

passenger (n)   a rider on the plane, a customer

schedule (n)   timetable, a plan that shows arrivals and departures

screen (n)   a "television" in the airport that shows the schedules

Idioms

Janet walked **in the direction of** the gate.   toward

Passengers only **at this point**.   right here

Did they **fix dinner**?   make or prepare dinner

We didn't want to **waste time**.   spend time in a bad way, lose time

Of course.   Sure. I understand.

Passengers Only at This Point

Janet was at the airport. She was there to pick up Ted and Mack. She wanted to be on time for the flight, so she arrived a little early. She wanted to check the flight schedule and be at the gate to meet Ted and Mack.

Janet parked her car in the parking lot, and walked into the airport. She looked for the flight schedule on the screen, but she didn't see it. So she walked to the airline counter and asked.

"Excuse me, but is Flight 244 from Dallas on time?"

"Yes, it is," answered the airline employee. "It's arriving at Gate 14."

Janet thanked the employee and walked in the direction of the gate. She wanted to wait at the gate, but an airport employee stopped her.

"Why can't I go to the gate?" Janet asked.

"I'm sorry," the employee answered. "Passengers only at this point. You must wait here."

Janet was a little upset, but there wasn't anything else to do. She waited there.

Then there was an announcement. Janet listened.

"The arrival for Flight 244 from Dallas is delayed. Flight 244 is delayed. Thank you."

"Oh, my gosh!" Janet shouted. "I didn't need to hurry."

Janet is waiting for Ted and Mack to arrive. Passengers begin to enter the waiting area. She sees Ted.

JANET: Ted! Ted! Here I am!

TED: Hi, honey. I missed you. How are you?

Ted gives Janet a big hug and kiss.

TED: Janet, this is Mack MacKay. We stayed at the hotel together.

JANET: Nice to meet you, Mack. I understand you need a ride home.

MACK: Yes, that's right. I'm glad you can help, Janet.

JANET: No problem. How was your flight? Did they serve you any dinner?

TED: No, they didn't. There wasn't any dinner on this flight.

JANET: Did you ask for a soda or anything?

MACK: Ted asked for a soda and I ordered a beer.

JANET: Well, are you two hungry? We can go out to a restaurant for dinner.

MACK: Thanks, Janet, but I'm tired, and I really miss my family. I'd like to go home right away.

JANET: Of course. I understand. Did you carry your bags on the plane?

MACK: Yes, we did. We didn't want to waste any extra time at the airport.

JANET: Okay, let's go.

Exercises

A. Answer the questions in complete sentences.

1. Where was Janet?

2. Why did she arrive a little early?

3. Where did she want to wait?

4. What did Janet listen to?

5. Did they serve any dinner?

6. What did Ted and Mack order?

7. What would Mack like?

8. What did Ted and Mack carry on the plane?

B. **True or false** Write **T** on the line if the sentence is true.
Write **F** on the line if the sentence is false.

_____ 1. If you waste time, you finish your work.

_____ 2. A flight is a trip on a bus.

_____ 3. A passenger can ride a plane, train or bus.

_____ 4. A schedule shows you arrival and departure times.

_____ 5. If you want to drink a soda on the plane, you can order
it.

_____ 6. If the gate number of an arrival is going to change,
somebody will make an announcement.

_____ 7. "Passengers only at this point" means that Janet can go to the gate to meet Ted.

_____ 8. Janet walked in the direction of the gate. This means that she walked to the parking lot.

C.   Past tense   Change each sentence to past tense. Follow the examples:

Janet parks the car.

Janet parked the car.

Janet doesn't park the car.

Janet didn't park the car.

1. Ted doesn't order a soda on the plane.

2. Janet doesn't arrive late.

3. They serve them dinner.

4. Mack misses his family.

5. The passengers don't carry their bags on the plane.

6. Mack orders a beer.

7. Janet hurries to the correct gate.

8. My friend and I want to be on time.

9. Janet doesn't see the flight schedule on the screen.

10. They don't serve dinner on this flight.

D. Any Complete each sentence with **any, anyone,** or **anything.** Follow the example:

Did they serve _____any_____ dinner?

1. Did Mack order _____ to drink?

2. Did Ted talk to _____ on the flight?

3. Janet was a little upset, but there wasn't _____ else to do.

4. I didn't see _____ screen in the airport.

5. There wasn't _____ dinner on the flight.

6. Did _____ meet him at the airport?

7. Did you order a soda or _____ ?

8. They didn't want to waste _____ extra time at the airport.

9. Ted and Mack didn't want _____ to eat.

10. I'd like a cola. Would you like to order _____ ?

E. **Flight schedules**   Look at this flight schedule and answer the questions.

ARRIVAL TIME	FROM	FLIGHT #	GATE	
1:55	Phoenix	244	12	On time
3:12	Chicago	963	15	On time
3:44	Dallas	789	14	Delayed

DEPARTURE TIME	TO	FLIGHT #	GATE	
11:46	Las Vegas	651	10	Boarding
12:13	San Francisco	788	9	Delayed
1:11	Seattle	442	13	On time

1. Which flight is arriving late? _____

2. What time does the flight for San Francisco leave?

   _____

3. If you're going to Las Vegas, at what gate do you catch your

   plane? _____

4. Where is Flight 442 going? _____

5. From what city is Flight 244 coming? _____

6. How many planes are late? _____

7. If your friend is coming from Dallas, what time will she

   arrive? _____

8. Your friend is coming from Phoenix. At what gate will he

   arrive? ⎯⎯⎯⎯⎯⎯

F. Short answer   Practice these exchanges with a partner.
Use **did** or **didn't** to give the correct past tense short answer.
Follow the example:

> **A:** Did they serve any dinner?
>
> **B:** No, ⎯⎯they didn't⎯⎯ . We didn't eat.

1. **A:** Did you order anything?

   B: Yes, ⎯⎯⎯⎯⎯⎯ . I ordered an orange juice.

2. **A:** Did you carry your bag on the plane?

   B: Yes, ⎯⎯⎯⎯⎯⎯ . I didn't want to waste any time at
   the airport.

3. **A:** Did Janet arrive on time?

   B: Yes, ⎯⎯⎯⎯⎯⎯ . She was on time.

4. **A:** Did you see the flight schedule?

   B: No, ⎯⎯⎯⎯⎯⎯ . I asked an airline employee.

5. **A:** Did Ted and Mack want to go to a restaurant?

   B: No, _____ . They wanted to go home.

6. **A:** Did the plane arrive on time?

   B: Yes, _____ . It arrived at Gate 14.

7. **A:** Did they thank you for the information?

   B: Yes, _____ . Ted and Janet thanked me.

8. **A:** Did the flight schedule change?

   B: No, _____ . It didn't change.

9. **A:** Did Ted and Mack waste any time at the airport?

   B: No, _____ . They carried their bags on the plane.

10. **A:** Did the flight arrive at Gate 12?

    B: No, _____ . It arrived at Gate 14.

CHAPTER 12

Go Straight and Turn Right

Vocabulary

attendant (n)   worker at a parking lot or gas station

hand (v)   give to

honk (v)   push the car horn

horn (n)   car instrument that makes a loud noise

lift (v)   raise, pull up

signal (v)   show that you're turning right or left

trunk (n)   the back of a car used for bags and suitcases

Idioms

That was a **close call**.   almost an accident

It's easy to **get to** my house.   reach, arrive

Go straight.   Don't turn right or left.

Give me **directions**.   tell the way to go

How fast are you going?   How fast are you driving?

Go Straight and Turn Right

Ted, Mack and Janet walked out of the airport and to the car. Mack handed his bag to Ted, and Ted lifted the bags into the trunk.

"Would you like to drive, Janet?" Ted asked. "I'm really tired from the flight."

"I'd be happy to drive, honey," Janet answered.

On the way out of the parking lot, Janet handed a dollar to the attendant. The dollar was for parking.

There was a lot of traffic at the airport that night. It was difficult for Janet to drive out of the airport area and reach her exit. She signaled for a right turn, then turned onto her exit. A driver behind Janet honked his horn.

"Wow! That was a close call, Janet! Be careful!" Ted shouted.

"Don't shout at me, Ted. It's hard to drive in this terrible traffic."

But now Ted was nervous. He wanted to drive.

"Do you want me to drive, Janet? Let me drive. You don't know where Mack lives. I'll drive."

"No way. I'm fine. Just give me directions," answered Janet. "Mack can help me. Right, Mack?"

"Sure, Janet. It's easy to get to my house. I'll help you with directions. No problem."

Now they're on the highway. Mack is giving Janet directions.

MACK: Stay on this road for a couple of miles.

TED: Janet! Be careful! There's a truck on your right!

JANET: Yes, Ted. I see it. Do I want this exit, Mack?

MACK: Don't take this exit, Janet. Take the next exit in two miles.

TED: Janet, how fast are you going? It's important to drive fifty-five.

JANET: I'm fine, Ted. Don't be nervous. Everything is okay.

MACK: This is the exit, Janet. Take it and turn left.

JANET: Are you sure, Mack? Is it okay to turn left here?

TED: Janet! Don't look at Mack! Look at the road!

JANET: Ted, it's impossible for me to drive! You're shouting!

TED: Do you want me to drive? I'll drive. Stop here. I'll drive.

MACK: Go straight and turn right at the stop sign. Then go three blocks and turn left.

JANET: Okay. Does your wife know you're coming home tonight? Did you call her?

MACK: Yes, I did. I called her from Dallas.

TED: Here, Janet! Turn here! This is the street!

JANET: I know, Ted. Take it easy.

MACK: Well, thanks for the ride. Do you two want to come in for a minute?

TED: No thanks, Mack. I'm really tired. I just want to go home.

JANET: 'Night, Mack.

Exercises

A. Answer the questions in complete sentences.

1. What did Mack hand to Ted?

2. What did Ted do with the bags?

3. What did Janet hand to the attendant?

4. What did the driver behind Janet do?

5. Who will help Janet with directions?

6. How fast is Janet going? (What do you think?)

7. From where did Mack call his wife?

8. What does Ted want to do?

B. Present/past questions Complete each sentence with the correct helping verb to make a question. Use **do, does** or **did**. Follow the example:

    <u>Does</u> your wife know you're coming home?

1. _____ you want me to drive? I can drive.

2. _____ Janet want to pick them up at the airport tonight?

3. _____ Ted and Mack go to Dallas last week?

4. _____ I go straight or turn right?

5. _____ Ted always shout at Janet in the car?

6. _____ they arrive last night?

7. _____ the employees fly to Dallas every year?

8. _____ the driver behind Janet honk his horn? Was he angry?

C.   Matching   Match each group of words in **A** with a group of words in **B** to make a complete sentence.

A	**B**
_____ 1. Go straight and	a. for a right turn.
_____ 2. It's easy to	b. give me directions.
_____ 3. Janet handed a dollar	c. in this terrible traffic.
_____ 4. How fast	d. into the trunk.
_____ 5. A driver behind her	e. get to my house.
_____ 6. I'm fine. Just	f. honked his horn.
_____ 7. Ted lifted the bags	g. to the attendant.
_____ 8. She signaled	h. a close call!
_____ 9. Wow! That was	i. turn right at the stop sign.
_____ 10. It's hard to drive	j. are you going?

D.   Impersonal expressions   Use each group of words to make a sentence beginning with **It's + adjective + infinitive.** Follow the example:

easy + get + to my house

It's easy to get to my house.

1. impossible + drive + in this terrible traffic

2. difficult + drive + out of the airport

3. important + go + fifty-five

4. okay + turn + left here

5. necessary + have + a driver's license

6. nice + see + you again

7. easy + give + directions + to Janet

8. necessary + pay + the attendant

9. great + be + home

10. nice + know + you missed me

E.   Short story   Complete each sentence with the correct tense of the verb. Use the present, past, and future tenses.

Ted, Mack and Janet <u>walked</u> out of the airport and to the car.
(1) walk

Ted _____ the bags into the trunk. Janet _____ a dollar to the
(2) lift   (3) hand

attendant. It _____ difficult for Janet to drive out of the airport
(4) be

area. Ted _____ nervous.
(5) be

    He asked, "Do you want me to drive? I _____ .
(6) drive

You _____ where Mack lives."
(7) not/know

    Mack answered, "It _____ easy to get to my house. I _____
(8) be   (9) give

you directions."

    Janet often _____ Ted up from the airport. Sometimes Janet
(10) pick

_____ . Sometimes Ted _____ to drive home.
(11) drive   (12) like

F. Dialogues Practice one of these dialogues with a partner.
Present it to the class.

Dialogue One

A: Would you like to drive? I'm really tired.

B: I'd be happy to drive

A: It's easy to get to my house.

B: Just give me directions.

A: Take the next exit and turn left.

B: Is it okay to turn left here?

Dialogue Two

A: Wow! That was a close call!

B: It's hard to drive in this terrible traffic.

A: Do you want me to drive?

B: No, I'm fine. Just give me directions.

A: Go straight for three blocks.

B: Is this the street?

Dialogue Three

A: I'm really tired from the flight.

B: No problem. I'll drive. Let's go.

A: Be careful! There's a truck on your right.

B: Yes, I see it. Take it easy.

A: How fast are you going?

B: I'm going fifty-five. Don't be nervous.

Dialogue Four

A: Do I want this exit?

B: No. Take the next exit in two miles.

A: Do I go straight at the stop sign?

B: No. Turn left and go three blocks.

A: Does your husband/wife know you're coming home?

B: Yes. I called him/her from Dallas.

Dialogue Five

A: Is this your house?

B: Yes, the red one on the right.

A: 'Night, Mack. Take it easy.

B: Okay, thanks for the ride.

CHAPTER 13

Onions Make You Snore

Vocabulary

scrambled eggs (n)   eggs that are mixed and cooked

slice (n)   piece, cut of something

snack (n)   a little food to eat between meals

snore (v)   make a loud noise in the throat when sleeping

soon (adv)   in a short period of time

spatula (n)   a kitchen tool used for turning eggs and pancakes

suitcase (n)   bag for clothes

Idioms

Take off your clothes.   remove

Put on your pajamas.   place on your body

Ted **tossed and turned** in bed.   moved a lot

Would you like **a few** onions?   three or four (used with plural nouns)

Would you like **a little** cheese?   some, not much (used with singular nouns)

Onions Make You Snore

"Ted, Ted. We're home, Ted." Janet needed to wake her husband up. He was asleep in the car. "We're home, honey. Wake up."

Ted opened his eyes. "What? Are we home from the airport?"

Janet helped Ted out of the car and into the apartment. He was so tired.

"Go and take off your clothes and put on your pajamas, honey. I'll take care of your suitcase." Janet opened the trunk and lifted Ted's bag out.

Ted walked into the bedroom. He opened his top drawer and looked for his pajamas. He didn't see them. He called to Janet, "Where are my pajamas, Janet? I can't find them."

"Oh, I'm sorry, Ted," she answered. "I didn't have time to wash the clothes this week. Here. Wear these." Janet handed Ted the pajamas from his suitcase.

Ted didn't wash his face and he didn't brush his teeth. He was so tired. Soon he started to snore.

Janet didn't take care of Ted's dirty clothes in the suitcase. She lifted the bag onto a chair. "That'll be okay. I'll take care of everything tomorrow." Janet was tired, too.

Soon Ted and Janet were asleep, but Ted tossed and turned in bed. First he pushed the blankets. Then he pulled the blankets. Then he pushed them again. In a few minutes, Janet was awake. She needed to wake her husband up again.

"Honey, wake up. Ted! Wake up!"

"What? What's the matter?" Ted asked. "What is it? Are we home from the airport?"

Now Ted and Janet are wide awake. They're in the kitchen. They want a midnight snack.

116

TED: Will you make something to eat, Janet? I didn't have dinner. I'm hungry.

JANET: How about scrambled eggs? I'll fix the eggs. You look for the frying pan and the spatula.

TED: Where are they? I can't find them.

JANET: The spatula is in the drawer next to the stove. The frying pan is dirty. Look in the sink. Will you wash it?

TED: Sure. Hey, would you like a few onions and a little cheese in the eggs? I like onions and cheese.

JANET: A little cheese is all right, but no onions. Onions make you snore.

TED: I'd like a little bacon, too. I'm hungry.

JANET: Oh, I'm sorry, Ted. I didn't go to the supermarket. We don't have any bacon. How about a few slices of fruit? There's a little melon in the refrigerator. It's in the drawer.

TED: Let's make a few pieces of toast. I'm really hungry.

JANET: Okay. Here's a knife. You slice the cheese and cut the fruit. Hand me the spatula. I'll fix the eggs and the toast.

TED: Super! This is a terrific midnight snack!

JANET: Snack! Are you kidding? This is breakfast!

Exercises

A.   Answer the questions in complete sentences.

1. What did Janet need to do to her husband?

2. What did Janet open and lift?

3. What did Janet hand Ted?

4. What didn't Ted wash?

5. What did Ted do in bed?

6. Where is the spatula?

7. What's in the refrigerator?

8. What will Janet fix?

B.   Take one out   Read each of the word groups. Take out the word or words that do not belong.

1. eggs, onions, snore, cheese

2. pajamas, tossed, turned, moved

3. snack, spatula, scrambled eggs, breakfast

4. wake up, put on, soon, take off

5. suitcase, bag, drawer, slice

6. midnight, knife, spatula, frying pan

C.   Few/a little   Complete each sentence with **a few** or **a little**. Follow the examples:

I have _____a little_____ time to help you.

I'd like _____a few_____ pieces of toast.

1. Are you hungry? How about _____ eggs?

2. There's _____ melon in the refrigerator.

3. Would you like _____ slices of fruit?

4. Let's have _____ snack.

5. I'd like _____ onions in my scrambled eggs.

6. How about _____ bacon? I'm really hungry.

7. Can we have _____ cheese in our eggs?

8. There are _____ dirty dishes in the sink.

D.   Negative past   Change each past tense sentence to the negative. Follow the example:

Ted looked for his pajamas.

Ted didn't look for his pajamas.

1. Janet lifted the bag out of the trunk.

2. Ted opened his eyes.

3. Janet handed Ted the pajamas from his suitcase.

4. I washed the dirty clothes.

5. Ted and Janet fixed a midnight snack.

6. Ted and I carried our bags on the plane.

7. Janet sliced the cheese.

8. I looked for the spatula.

9. We wanted onions in our scrambled eggs.

10. Ted snored.

E.   A midnight snack   Make an omelet. Read each sentence. What do you want to do next? Use numbers 3 through 8 to put the sentences in order.

_____ Wash and peel the onion.

_1_ Get the spatula, frying pan, eggs, onion, cheese and butter.

_____ Turn on the stove and put butter in the pan.

_____ Put the eggs in the frying pan.

_____ Chop the onion and the cheese.

_____ Serve with toast and jelly.

_____ Add the onion and cheese.

_2_ Beat the eggs.

F. Talk about a midnight snack with a partner.

A: I didn't have dinner. I'm _____ .

B: Would you like a midnight _____ ?

A: Super! How about _____ ?

B: Okay. You look for the _____ and the _____ .

A: Would you like a few _____ and a little _____ in the _____ ?

B: Oh, I'm sorry. I didn't go to the _____ . We don't have any _____ .

A: Well, let's make a few pieces of _____ . Anything else?

B: I think there's a little melon in the _____ .

A: Super! This is a terrific _____ !

B: Snack! Are you kidding? This is _____ !

CHAPTER 14

At the Amusement Park

Vocabulary

admission gate (n)   entrance of an amusement park or zoo

amusement park (n)   a large park with rides and entertainment

freeway (n)   highway

parade (n)   a march down the middle of the street

relax (v)   take it easy

ride (n)   a roller coaster or Ferris wheel

shuttle bus (n)   a bus that takes people from the parking lot to the admission gate

Idioms

They planned to spend **all day** there.   from morning to evening

Two dollars **apiece**.   each, each one

Did you **raise** your **prices**?   make the prices higher

You can ride **free of charge**.   free, no fee

Have fun.   Enjoy yourself.

I see.   I understand.

At the Amusement Park

Ted and Janet worked hard. They went to work all week, and they cleaned house on the weekend. They wanted to take a break, and they wanted to have some fun. So Ted and Janet planned to go to an amusement park on Sunday. They planned to arrive early and spend all day there.

That Sunday, Ted and Janet were on the freeway early in the morning. It was easy to drive because there wasn't much traffic on the road. There weren't many cars and there weren't many trucks. But there was a small accident. Janet saw it.

"Be careful, Ted. There's an accident ahead. Slow down."

"Don't worry, Janet. I'm fine," Ted answered.

They continued on the freeway for many miles. They didn't talk. Ted watched the road, and Janet looked out the window. In about two hours, they arrived at Super Family Fun Park. Ted parked the car, and they waited for the shuttle bus to take them to the admission gate.

There weren't many people there yet, but Ted and Janet needed to stand in line because the ticket windows weren't open.

"We're nice and early. We won't need to stand in long lines for our first few rides, Janet. That's great. Did you remember the discount coupon?" Ted asked.

"Yes, I did," Janet answered. "I have it in my purse."

They waited in line for fifteen minutes. Then the admission windows opened.

TED: Two, please. And I have this coupon.

CASHIER: Let me see. All right. That gives you two dollars off the regular admission price.

TED: Is that two dollars off each?

CASHIER: Yes, sir. Two dollars off apiece. Thirty-eight dollars, please.

TED: Thirty-eight dollars? Wow! Did you raise your prices?

CASHIER: Yes, we did. But please remember that you can spend all day inside the park and ride every ride free of charge. You only pay at the stores and restaurants.

TED: I see. Okay. Thirty-eight dollars. Here you are.

CASHIER: Thank you, sir. Have fun at Super Family Fun Park.

Ted and Janet walked around Super Family Fun Park all day. They enjoyed the rides, listened to the bands, saw a parade, watched some shows, shopped in the stores and used all their money. Now they're tired and ready to go home.

TED: Did you enjoy yourself, Janet?

JANET: Yes, I did. I enjoyed every minute. It was lucky that we arrived early. There weren't many people in line for the rides.

TED: Did you enjoy your meal? You didn't eat much lunch.

JANET: It was okay, but it was a little expensive.

TED: I don't care. We needed a nice day to relax. It was great.

JANE: Right. Let's go home. I'm tired.

TED: Me too. Hey, Janet. Did you remember my Super Family Fun hat and my Super Family Fun T-shirt?

JANET: Yes honey, I did. I have them in my purse.

Exercises

A.   Answer the questions in complete sentences.

1. Where did Ted and Janet plan to go on Sunday?

2. Why was it easy to drive?

3. In the parking lot, what did they wait for?

4. Why did Ted and Janet need to stand in line at the ticket windows?

5. How long did they wait?

6. How much were the tickets?

7. What did Ted and Janet listen to?

8. What did Ted and Janet see?

B.   **Multiple choice**   Choose **a**, **b** or **c** as the correct answer.

1. A freeway is _____ .

    a. a highway

    b. a discount coupon

    c. a ride at an amusement park

2. Free of charge means _____ .

    a. Two dollars off

    b. you don't need to pay

    c. you don't need to stand in line

3. Ted asked, "Did you enjoy yourself?" This means _____ .

    a. Did you understand the price?

    b. Did you ride the shuttle bus?

    c. Did you have fun?

4. Ted and Janet waited in line for fifteen minutes because _____ .

    a. they were late

    b. Super Family Fun Park was closed for a holiday

    c. the admission gates weren't open

5. Ted parked the car. What did they wait for? They waited for _____ .

    a. rides inside the amusement park

    b. the shuttle bus

    c. the parade

6. Ted asked, "Did you raise your prices?" This means: _____ .

    a. Did your prices go higher?

    b. Do you accept discount coupons?

    c. Can I pay thirty-eight dollars?

7. They needed a nice day to relax means _____ .

    a. they needed to use all their money

    b. they needed to ride the rides free of charge

    c. they needed to take a break

8. The cashier tells Ted, "Two dollars off apiece." This means
   _____ .

   a. Ted and Janet will pay regular price

   b. Ted and Janet will save four dollars

   c. Ted and Janet will stand in line for fifteen minutes

C. Past tense questions   Change each of these negative
sentences to a question. Follow the example:

He didn't have fun. __Did he have__ fun?

1. She didn't see the parade. _____ she _____ the parade?

2. They didn't need to stand in line. _____ they _____ to
   stand in line?

3. I didn't remember the coupon. _____ you _____ the
   coupon?

4. Ted and Janet didn't see many people. _____ many
   people?

5. We didn't plan to go to Super Family Fun Park. (you)

   _____ to go to Super Family Fun Park?

6. They didn't arrive early. _____ early?

7. The admission gate didn't open at nine. _____ at
   nine?

8. I didn't look out the window. (you) _____ out the window?

9. He didn't wait for the shuttle bus. _____ for the shuttle bus?

10. Janet didn't like her lunch. _____ her lunch?

D.   Much/many   Complete each sentence with **much** or **many**. Follow the example:

They didn't have __much__ fun.

1. Ted and Janet didn't talk for _____ miles.

2. I didn't see _____ cars on the road.

3. Janet didn't carry _____ money in her purse.

4. They arrived _____ hours later.

5. There weren't _____ people at the admission gate.

6. There wasn't _____ traffic on the freeway.

7. We saw _____ different shows at Super Family Fun Park.

8. Janet didn't eat _____ lunch.

9. We didn't ride on _____ rides.

10. Ted and Janet don't have _____ days off.

E. Admissions Look at the admissions sign below. Then complete each sentence.

```
┌─────────────────────────────────────────────┐
│                                             │
│        SUPER FAMILY FUN PARK                │
│                                             │
│    Adults.......................... $21.00   │
│                                             │
│    Children 3–12 ................. $15.75    │
│                                             │
│    Children under 3................ FREE     │
│                                             │
│    Seniors (55 and older)......... $17.50    │
│                                             │
│    Coupons and groups .....Gates 7 & 8       │
│                                             │
└─────────────────────────────────────────────┘
```

1. Ted and Janet have coupons. They need to go to Gate _____ .

2. A sixty-year-old man is taking his grandson to the amusement park. The boy is fourteen. The man pays _____ for the tickets.

3. Children _____ can enter free of charge.

4. A family of two adults and a ten-year-old child will pay _____ to enter the park.

5. A teacher and her class must buy tickets at _____ .

6. A fifty-four-year-old woman will pay _____ for her ticket.

7. A group of ten seniors will pay a total of _____ for their admission.

8. With a coupon for three dollars off each, an adult couple will pay _____ for their admission.

F. Ask your partner Practice asking and answering questions with a partner. Read these instructions and ask the correct questions. Your partner must answer in complete sentences. Then, have your partner ask you the questions.

1. Ask where he or she went last Sunday. (Where did . . . ?)

2. Ask what he or she saw there. (What did . . . ?)

3. Ask if he or she went to an amusement park last summer. (Did you . . . ?)

4. Ask if he or she arrived at school early. (Did you . . . ?)

5. Ask if he or she cleaned his or her house last weekend. (Did you . . . ?)

6. Ask what time he or she finished his or her housework. (What time did . . . ?)

7. Ask where he or she went on his or her last vacation. (Where did . . . ?)

8. Ask what he or she saw there. (What did . . . ?)

9. Ask where he or she went for his or her last birthday. (Where did . . .?)

10. Ask what he or she saw there. (What did . . .?)

CHAPTER 15

A Couple of Minutes Before Midnight

In this chapter you will recognize many of the vocabulary words and idioms that were introduced in chapters 1 through 14. The exercises will help you review grammar, vocabulary, and idioms.

As you complete the exercises, see if you can remember the situation in which a vocabulary word or idiom was first used. Think about the different events that occur in this novel.

Before you read this final chapter, think about the title "A Couple of Minutes Before Midnight." Look at the picture of Ted and Janet. What do you think the title refers to? Discuss what you think will happen in this chapter with a partner.

A Couple of Minutes
Before Midnight

Many weeks ago, Ted and Janet decided to have a New Year's Eve party. They invited a few friends from work and a few neighbors.

There were so many things that Ted and Janet needed to do for the party. They needed to clean the apartment, shop for snacks and prepare a dinner. They also wanted to serve champagne at midnight because they wanted to toast the new year.

Janet's cleaning the apartment now. She'd like Ted to go to the supermarket and shop for the products they need. She asks, "Would you like to go shopping, Ted? I'm really very busy."

"No problem. I'll go," Ted answers. "I'll be back in an hour."

"Don't forget the coupons. And there's a little money in my purse." Ted went shopping and Janet cleaned house.

Janet's vacuuming now, and soon she's going to fix the snacks and prepare the dinner.

Soon Ted walks in with many bags of groceries.

"Hi, Janet. I'm back. I shopped for everything, but I didn't see that white cheese. I picked out this cheddar, okay? And I checked out the veggies. I saw sales on carrots, cucumbers and broccoli. We can make a tray of veggies. Are you ready to take a break?"

"No. I'm going to finish this mess in the kitchen."

"All right," Ted answers. "I'll take a nap for a couple of hours. I need to relax."

"No way, Ted!" Janet shouts. "It's impossible for me to finish everything for the party. You need to help me. We're running late, and I'm in a hurry."

Ted saw the mess in the kitchen. He didn't waste any time. He helped Janet, and he worked fast.

Now their friends and neighbors are at the party. Everyone is having fun. People are all over the apartment.

FRIEND: Hi, Janet. Nice party. Did you stay home all day and work? Your place is so neat and clean. And you fixed so much stuff to eat! Thank you.

JANET: My pleasure. I enjoy it. It's a lot of work, but I don't care.

NEIGHBOR: Hi, Ted. How's it going? Pretty good? Are you tired of married life yet? Ha-ha.

TED: Are you kidding? It's great to be married. There isn't anything wrong with my life!

NEIGHBOR: I'm divorced. Sometimes I miss my kids. Maybe I'll call them now. May I use your telephone? I'll call collect. I think my ex-wife will accept the charges.

TED: Of course. Go ahead. There's a phone in the bedroom.

A couple of minutes before midnight, Ted and Janet asked everyone to keep still. They didn't want anyone to talk. Ted and Janet wanted to toast the new year. Now it is midnight.

JANET: To my husband and to our friends and neighbors. Happy New Year!

TED: And to a very, very wonderful future for everyone! Happy New Year!

Exercises

A.   Answer the questions in complete sentences.

1. What did Ted and Janet decide many weeks ago?

2. What did they want to serve at midnight?

3. Janet cleaned the house. Where did Ted go?

4. On what did Ted see sales?

5. What did Ted see in the kitchen?

6. Why did Ted and Janet ask everyone to keep still?

B.   Review of idioms   Find the sentence in **A** that has the same meaning as the sentence in **B**. Write the letter of the correct answer on the line.

A	**B**
_____ 1. Are you tired of married life?	a. She'll pay for the call.
_____ 2. He always picks out that cheese.	b. He examined the vegetables.
_____ 3. We're running late.	c. People are everywhere.
_____ 4. She'll accept the charges.	d. I'm happy to help.
_____ 5. Everyone is having fun.	e. How are you?
_____ 6. He checked out the veggies.	f. We're in a hurry.

_____ 7. I'll be back in an hour.

g. Ted chooses cheddar.

_____ 8. People are all over the apartment.

h. They wanted everyone to be quiet.

_____ 9. How's it going?

i. Everyone is enjoying the party.

_____ 10. It's my pleasure.

j. Are you bored with married life?

_____ 11. They wanted everyone to keep still.

k. It was two minutes before midnight.

_____ 12. It was a couple of minutes before midnight.

l. I'll return soon.

C. Grammar review   Underline the correct answer.

1. Ted and Janet (needed/needed to) clean the apartment.

2. Janet's (vacuums/vacuuming) now.

3. He'll (be back/is back) in an hour.

4. There (is/are) money in her purse.

5. Sometimes he (miss/misses) his kids.

6. I didn't (see/saw) that white cheese.

7. Are you (go/going) to finish the kitchen?

8. Janet (would like/like) Ted to go to the supermarket.

9. They invited (a little/a few) friends and neighbors.

10. There were so (much/many) things that they needed for the party.

11. It's impossible for Janet (to finish/finishing) everything for the party.

12. Ted (seeing/saw) the mess in the kitchen.

13. There wasn't (anything/something) wrong with Ted's life.

14. They wanted to serve (a few/a little) champagne.

15. Janet (didn't finish/didn't finished) the laundry.

16. (Don't forget/Won't forget) the coupons, please.

17. "No problem," Ted (answering/answers).

18. (Do/Can/Are) you want champagne?

19. I think she'll (accept/accepting) the charges.

20. Do you want (invite/to invite) the neighbors?

D. Short story   Complete each sentence with the correct form of the verb. Use present, present continuous, **going to** future or past.

Many weeks ago, Ted and Janet _____ to have a New Year's
                                    (1) decide

Eve party. They _____ a few friends and neighbors. Right now
                (2) invite

Janet _____ the apartment. Soon she _____ snacks.
      (3) clean   (4) fix

Before the party, Ted _____ shopping. He _____ sales on
                      (5) go   (6) see

carrots, cucumbers and broccoli. He also _____ out some
(7) pick

cheddar cheese.

Right now Ted and Janet _____ a tray of veggies. Soon their
(8) fix

friends and neighbors _____ .
(9) arrive

Everyone _____ at the party now, and everyone _____ fun.
(10) be   (11) have

A neighbor _____ Janet, "Did you stay home all day and work?
(12) ask

Your place is so neat and clean!"

Janet answers, "Well, I _____ it. It's a lot of work, but I
(13) enjoy

_____ ."
(14) not/care

E. Word order   Make a sentence or a question by putting the words in the correct order.

1. to / like / you / Would / shopping / go

2. champagne / wanted / They / serve / midnight / to / at

3. break / you / a / take / ready / Are / to

4. impossible / everything / finish / to / It's / me / for

5. to / and / keep / Ted / everyone / still / Janet / asked

6. invited / few / work / friends / They / from / a

7. finish / mess / kitchen / I'm / to / this / going / the / in

8. telephone / I / your / use / May

9. don't / lot / care / but / I / It's / a / of / work

10. time / waste / didn't / He / any

F. Ask your partner   Practice asking and answering questions with a partner. Read the instructions and ask the correct questions. Your partner must answer in complete sentences. Then, have your partner ask you the questions.

1. Ask if he or she likes to go to New Year's Eve parties. (Do you . . . ?)

2. Ask where he or she went last New Year's Eve. (Where did you . . . ?)

3. Ask what he or she saw there. (What did . . . ?)

4. Ask what he or she picked out at the supermarket last week. (What did . . . ?)

5. Ask if he or she used coupons. (Did you . . . ?)

6. Ask if he or she saw any sales. (Did you . . . ?)

7. Ask if he or she is going to have a party next weekend. (Are you . . . ?)

8. Ask if he or she is going to stay home next weekend. (Are you . . . ?)

9. Ask how often he or she goes to parties. (How often do . . . ?)

10. Ask if he or she is having fun now. (Are you . . . ?)

NTC ESL/EFL TEXTS AND MATERIAL
Junior High—Adult Education

Computer Software
Amigo
Basic Vocabulary Builder on Computer

Language and Culture Readers
Beginner's English Reader
Advanced Beginner's English Reader
Cultural Encounters in the U.S.A.
Passport to America Series
  California Discovery
  Adventures in the Southwest
  The Coast-to-Coast Mystery
  The New York Connection
Discover America Series
  California, Chicago, Florida, Hawaii,
  New England, New York, Texas,
  Washington, D.C.
Looking at America Series
  Looking at American Signs, Looking at
  American Food, Looking at American
  Recreation, Looking at American Holidays
Time: We the People
Communicative American English
English á la Cartoon

Text/Audiocassette Learning Packages
Speak Up! Sing Out!
Listen and Say It Right in English!

Transparencies
Everyday Situations in English

**Duplicating Masters and
Black-line Masters**
The Complete ESL/EFL Cooperative and
  Communicative Activity Book
Easy Vocabulary Games
Vocabulary Games
Advanced Vocabulary Games
Play and Practice!
Basic Vocabulary Builder
Practical Vocabulary Builder
Beginning Activities for English
  Language Learners
Intermediate Activities for English
  Language Learners
Advanced Activities for English
  Language Learners

Language-Skills Texts
Starting English with a Smile
English with a Smile
More English with a Smile
English Survival Series
  Building Vocabulary, Recognizing Details,
  Identifying Main Ideas, Writing Sentences
  and Paragraphs, Using the Context
English Across the Curriculum
Essentials of Reading and Writing English
Everyday English
Everyday Situations for Communicating in
  English
Learning to Listen in English
Listening to Communicate in English
Communication Skillbooks
Living in the U.S.A.
Basic English Vocabulary Builder Activity Book
Basic Everyday Spelling Workbook
Practical Everyday Spelling Workbook

Advanced Readings and Communicative
  Activities for Oral Proficiency
Practical English Writing Skills
Express Yourself in Written English
Campus English
English Communication Skills for Professionals
Speak English!
Read English!
Write English!
Orientation in American English
Building English Sentences
Grammar for Use
Grammar Step-by-Step
Listening by Doing
Reading by Doing
Speaking by Doing
Vocabulary by Doing
Writing by Doing
Look, Think and Write

Life- and Work-Skills Texts
English for Success
Building Real Life English Skills
Everyday Consumer English
Book of Forms
Essential Life Skills series
Finding a Job in the United States
English for Adult Living
Living in English
Prevocational English

TOEFL and University Preparation
NTC's Preparation Course for the TOEFL®
NTC's Practice Tests for the TOEFL®
How to Apply to American Colleges
  and Universities
The International Student's Guide
  to the American University

Dictionaries and References
ABC's of Languages and Linguistics
Everyday American English Dictionary
Building Dictionary Skills in
  English (workbook)
Beginner's Dictionary of American
  English Usage
Beginner's English Dictionary
  Workbook
NTC's American Idioms Dictionary
NTC's Dictionary of American Slang
  and Colloquial Expressions
NTC's Dictionary of Phrasal Verbs
NTC's Dictionary of Grammar Terminology
Essential American Idioms
Contemporary American Slang
Forbidden American English
101 American English Idioms
101 American English Proverbs
Practical Idioms
Essentials of English Grammar
The Complete ESL/EFL Resource Book
Safari Grammar
Safari Punctuation
303 Dumb Spelling Mistakes
TESOL Professional Anthologies
  Grammar and Composition
  Listening, Speaking, and Reading
  Culture

For further information or a current catalog, write:
National Textbook Company
a division of NTC Publishing Group
4255 West Touhy Avenue
Lincolnwood, Illinois 60646-1975 U.S.A.